... when you need it in writing! ®

301
Legal Forms and Agreements

to safeguard your legal rights and protect you...
your family... your property...and your business
from everyday legal problems.

compiled by
Mario D. German, Esquire

edited by
Sondra Servais

E·Z LEGAL BOOKS®

384 South Military Trail, Deerfield Beach, FL 33442
phone: (954) 480-8933 • fax: (954) 480-8906

… when you need it in writing!

E-Z Legal Forms, Inc.
384 S. Military Trail
Deerfield Beach FL 33442

Distributed by E-Z Legal Forms, Inc.

Manufactured in the United States of America

5 6 7 8 9 10   80960

This book is sold with the understanding that neither the author nor the publisher is engaged in rendering legal advice. If legal advice is required, the services of an attorney should be sought. Publisher and author cannot in any way guarantee that the forms in this book are being used for the purposes intended and, therefore, assume no responsibility for their proper and correct use.

Library of Congress Catalog Card Number: 93-72019

301 Legal Forms and Agreements
  Compiled by Mario D. German, Esquire.
  Sondra Servais, editor.
        p.   cm.
  ISBN 1-56382-301-2: $24.95
I. German, Mario D., compiled by. II. Servais, Sondra, edited by. III.
Title: 301 Legal Forms and Agreements.

IMPORTANT FACTS

E-Z Legal Products are designed to provide authoritative and accurate information in regard to the subject matter covered. However, neither this nor any other publication can take the place of an attorney on important legal matters.

Information in this book has been carefully compiled from sources believed to be reliable, but the accuracy of the information is not guaranteed, as laws and regulations may change or be subject to differing interpretations. Additionally, certain courts may have their own requirements. Before completing and filing the forms in this book, you may want to check with the clerk of the court concerning these requirements.

Why not have your attorney review this book? We encourage it.

E•Z LEGAL FORMS®

384 S. Military Trail
Deerfield Beach, FL 33442
Tel. (954) 480-8933   Fax (954) 480-8906

About 301 Legal Forms...

This book contains all the important—and ready-to-complete legal forms and agreements that can safeguard your legal rights and protect you... your family... your property... and your business from everyday legal problems.

With 301 vital legal documents, you now have instantly available to you the protection you need without the inconvenience or cost of using an attorney for simple legal matters you can easily handle yourself.

E-Z Legal Forms is the ideal way to "get it in writing." What better way is there to legally document your important transactions, avoid troublesome disputes and enforce your legal rights? In moments you can have just the legal form or agreement you need to sidestep misunderstandings and costly lawsuits, comply with legal obligations and avoid liability.

Written by a panel of attorneys and law professors, E-Z Legal Forms have been certified as safe and effective for consumer use.

How to use E-Z Legal Forms...

You can easily and conveniently use 301 Legal Forms by following these simple instructions.

1 To find the appropriate form, you can check the two tables of contents. The first lists each form alphabetically. The second groups them in categories. In addition, each index contains a cross-reference to our *301 Legal Forms* software.

2 You may find several forms for the same general purpose, so review and select the form most appropriate for your specific needs. Use the Glossary, in the back of this book, as a guide to the purpose of each form.

3 Each form is perforated for easy removal and use. Photocopy and store the original so it can be used again in the future.

4 Fully complete each form. Make certain all blanks (name, address, dates, amounts) are filled in. Delete, modify or add provisions as required. Attach a separate addendum if additional terms cannot be easily inserted. All changes or addendums should be initialed by all parties. Verbal terms are generally not enforceable, so make certain your document includes all that was agreed upon.

5 Correspondence forms can be personalized by reproducing on your letterhead.

6 Some forms have footnoted instructions, which should be observed if you are to use the form properly.

7 The pronoun "it" within a form can properly refer to an individual as well as a business entity.

8 Important correspondence should always be delivered by certified mail, return receipt requested.

9 Use caution and common sense when using E-Z Legal Forms—or any other do-it-yourself legal product. While these forms are generally considered appropriate for self-use, you must nevertheless decide when you should instead seek professional legal advice. You should certainly consult an attorney when:

- You need a complex or important agreement.
- Your transaction involves substantial amounts of money or expensive property.
- You don't understand how to use a document—or question its adequacy to fully protect you.

Because we cannot be certain that the forms in this book are appropriate to your circumstances—or are being properly used—we cannot assume any liability or responsibility in connection with their use.

Table of Contents (Alphabetical)

—A—

—B—

—C—

—D—

—E—

—F—

—G—

—I—

—L—

—*M*—

—*N*—

—O—

—P—

—S—

—T—

—U—

—V—

—W—

Table of Contents (Categorical)
I. Basic Agreements

II. *Loans & Borrowing*

III. *Employment*

IV. *Credit & Collection*

V. Buying/Selling

VI. Leases & Tenancies

VII. *Transfers & Assignments*

VIII. *Personal & Family*

IX. *Real Estate*

X. *Business*

XI. Other Legal Forms

ACCEPTANCE OF CLAIM

Date:

To:

               Receipt   is   acknowledged   of   your   claim   against

for $ _____ . Your claim is accepted for collection under the following terms and conditions:

Our experience or contacts with the debtor are shown by check marks preceding the appropriate statements:

_____1. Personal demand is being made upon the debtor. A further report will be made to you in

         days.

_____2. The debtor is slow in payment, but we believe that we can collect your claim without

         suit.

_____3. The debtor must be sued. If you desire suit to be filed, please send duplicate invoices,

         statements of account, and the enclosed affidavit, properly executed, together with your

         check for $ _____ for advance court costs and suit fee. In the meantime, we

         shall try to effect an amicable settlement.

_____4. The debtor generally remits payment to the creditor immediately on our demand. Kindly

         advise us of direct remittances.

_____5. The debtor is in bankruptcy. Please execute the enclosed proof of claim and power of

         attorney and return them to us at once.

_____6. We have had _____ claims against the debtor and have collected on

         of them.

_____7. We now have _____ claims against the debtor and are collecting them by

         .

_____8. This debtor disputes the claim. Please furnish additional information concerning the claim and send us all original correspondence, together with any original orders, written acknowledgements, or promises to pay.

_____9. This debtor is out of business. The debtor has no property that can be levied on, and the debtor is not earning sufficient wages for garnishment. However, we believe the debtor will pay when possible. We will try to persuade the debtor to pay and shall keep you advised unless you advise us to return the claim to you.

Very truly,

_____

ACCIDENT CLAIM NOTICE

Date:

To:

Dear

You are hereby notified of a claim against you for damages arising from the following accident or injury, to which I believe you and/or your agents are liable.

Description of Accident:

Date:

Time:

Location:

Please have your insurance representative or attorney contact me as soon as possible.

Very truly,

_____
Name

_____
Address

_____

_____
Telephone

ACKNOWLEDGEMENT OF
MODIFIED TERMS

Date:

To:

Dear

Reference is made to the contract or order between us dated   , 19   .

This letter will acknowledge that the contract or order is modified and superseded by the following agreed change in terms:

All other terms shall remain as stated.

Unless we immediately hear from you to the contrary, in writing, we shall assume said modification is mutually agreeable, and we shall proceed accordingly on the modified terms. Please acknowledge same below and return one copy for our file.

Very truly,

_____

The foregoing modification is acknowledged:

_____

ADDENDUM TO CONTRACT

Reference is made to a certain agreement by and between the undersigned parties, said agreement being dated   , 19   (Contract).

BE IT KNOWN, that for good consideration the parties make the following additions or changes a part of said contract as if contained therein:

All other terms and provisions of said contract shall remain in full force and effect.

Signed this   day of   , 19   .

In the presence of:

_____   _____
Witness   First Party

_____   _____
Witness   Second Party

ADDRESS CHANGE NOTICE

Date:

To:

Dear

      Please be advised that effective   , 19   , our address has been changed from:

_____

_____

to

_____

_____

      Our new telephone number is:

      Please make note of the above information and direct all correspondence to us at our new address. Thank you.

_____

AFFIDAVIT

BE IT ACKNOWLEDGED, that

of _____ the undersigned

deponent, being of legal age, does hereby depose and say under oath as follows:

And I affirm that the foregoing is true except as to statements made upon information and

belief, and as to those I believe them to be true.

Witness my hand under the penalties of perjury this _____ day of _____, 19 ___.

_____
Name

_____
Address

_____

STATE OF _____ ⎫
COUNTY OF _____ ⎭

On _____ before me, _____, personally appeared
_____, personally known to me (or
proved to me on the basis of satisfactory evidence) to be the person(s) whose name(s) is/are
subscribed to the within instrument and acknowledged to me that he/she/they executed the same
in his/her/their authorized capacity(ies), and that by his/her/their signature(s) on the instrument
the person(s), or the entity upon behalf of which the person(s) acted, executed the instrument.
WITNESS my hand and official seal.

Signature_____

Affiant _____Known _____Unknown
ID Produced_____
(Seal)

AFFIDAVIT OF LOST STOCK CERTIFICATE

The undersigned, being of lawful age, first being duly sworn, on oath states:

1.   That the undersigned is the record owner of   shares of the stock of

                    , (Corporation) as same appears on the books and

records of the Corporation as certificate number(s)   .

2.   The undersigned has made a due and diligent search for said stock certificate(s) but has

lost or misplaced same. The undersigned warrants and represents that said stock certificate has

not been sold, pledged or transferred.

3.   As an inducement for the Corporation issuing a duplicate replacement certificate, the

undersigned agrees to fully indemnify and save harmless the Corporation for any claim of

ownership by an asserted owner or holder of said original shares.

4.   Should said lost shares be located they shall promptly be returned and surrendered to the

Corporation.

5.   Upon demand by the Corporation, the undersigned shall post sufficient surety bond in

favor of the Corporation to indemnify the Corporation for any adverse claim thereto.

        Signed under seal this   day of   , 19   .

_____

STATE OF   }
COUNTY OF   }

On   before me,   , personally appeared
                               , personally known to me (or
proved to me on the basis of satisfactory evidence) to be the person(s) whose name(s) is/are
subscribed to the within instrument and acknowledged to me that he/she/they executed the same
in his/her/their authorized capacity(ies), and that by his/her/their signature(s) on the instrument
the person(s), or the entity upon behalf of which the person(s) acted, executed the instrument.
WITNESS my hand and official seal.

Signature_____

                              Affiant   _____Known   _____Unknown
                              ID Produced_____
                                                                (Seal)

AFFIDAVIT OF MAILING OF NOTICE
OF ANNUAL MEETING

STATE OF

COUNTY OF   }

I,   , being duly sworn accordingly by law, do hereby depose and say:

I am the Secretary of   , and that on the day of the month of   , in the year   , I personally deposited copies of the aforesaid notice of annual meeting in a post-office box in the City of   , State of   , prepaid postage.

Each copy of the notice was in a securely sealed and stamped envelope. One copy was addressed to each person whose name appears on the attached list and to respective addresses as shown on the list.

_____
Secretary

On   before me,   , personally appeared   , personally known to me (or proved to me on the basis of satisfactory evidence) to be the person(s) whose name(s) is/are subscribed to the within instrument and acknowledged to me that he/she/they executed the same in his/her/their authorized capacity(ies), and that by his/her/their signature(s) on the instrument the person(s), or the entity upon behalf of which the person(s) acted, executed the instrument. WITNESS my hand and official seal.

Signature_____

Affiant _____Known _____Unknown
ID Produced_____
(Seal)

AFFIDAVIT OF NOTICE BY MAIL

I, _____ , of _____ , first being sworn, say:

1. Affiant is a citizen and resident of the City of _____ ,
County of _____ , State of _____ , and is over the age of _____ years. Affiant is
neither interested in nor a party to the matter referred to in the copy of the notice attached hereto.

2. Affiant mailed a notice by _____ mail, with return receipt requested
by enclosing such notice in a sealed envelope with the postage thereon fully prepaid.

3. The notice was mailed on _____ , 19 _____ , at the post office located at
_____ . The notice was addressed to _____ and sent
to _____ . A true and complete copy of the notice is attached hereto and
incorporated herein by reference.

3. There was regular communication by the United States mail between the place of
mailing and the destination at the time of the mailing of the aforementioned notice.

Date:

_____

STATE OF _____ }
COUNTY OF _____

On _____ before me, _____ , personally appeared
_____ , personally known to me (or
proved to me on the basis of satisfactory evidence) to be the person(s) whose name(s) is/are
subscribed to the within instrument and acknowledged to me that he/she/they executed the same
in his/her/their authorized capacity(ies), and that by his/her/their signature(s) on the instrument
the person(s), or the entity upon behalf of which the person(s) acted, executed the instrument.
WITNESS my hand and official seal.

Signature_____

Affiant _____Known _____Unknown
ID Produced_____
(Seal)

AFFIDAVIT OF PUBLICATION OF CERTIFICATE–
FICTITIOUS OR ASSUMED NAME

STATE OF
COUNTY OF   }

, affiant, of   , City of
, County of   , State of   ,
being duly sworn on oath, deposes and says:

    1. Affiant is or was the   of   ,
a daily newspaper of general circulation, printed, published, and circulated in the City of
      , County of   , State of   .

    2. The original or renewal   name certificate, a true copy of which is
attached hereto and marked as Exhibit A, was published in said newspaper once a   for
      successive   , on the following dates:

and the publication was made in the newspaper proper and not in a supplement.

Dated: _____

On   before me,   , personally appeared
      , personally known to me (or
proved to me on the basis of satisfactory evidence) to be the person(s) whose name(s) is/are
subscribed to the within instrument and acknowledged to me that he/she/they executed the same
in his/her/their authorized capacity(ies), and that by his/her/their signature(s) on the instrument
the person(s), or the entity upon behalf of which the person(s) acted, executed the instrument.
WITNESS my hand and official seal.

Signature_____

                               Affiant   _____Known   _____Unknown
                               ID Produced_____
                                                    (Seal)

AGREEMENT OF WAIVER OF RIGHT OF INHERITANCE

THIS AGREEMENT, made _____ , 19 ___ , by and between _____ (Husband) and _____ (Wife).

1.   Recital. Husband and wife have each been previously married and have children by prior marriages. Husband desires that his children shall inherit his property, and Wife desires that her children shall inherit her property.

2.   Waiver and Release. Accordingly, in consideration of our mutual promises and other valuable consideration, husband and wife waive any statutory or intestate right or interest that he or she has or may at any time have in any property now owned or subsequently acquired by the other. Each of the parties releases the other and his or her estate from any and all intestate interest, right, or distributive share that he or she may otherwise be entitled to on the death of the other, and waives the right to elect to take against any will or codicil made by the other that may be offered for or admitted to probate. The parties agree not to oppose but to permit the admission to probate of any will of the other, and to permit the other's estate to be administered by the person or persons legally entitled to do so as if we were not married.

_____   _____
Witness   Witness

IN WITNESS WHEREOF, we have subscribed our names on the day and year set forth.

_____   _____
Husband   Wife

AGREEMENT TO ASSUME OBLIGATION
SECURED BY MORTGAGE

The undersigned, _____ , in consideration of forbearance of

_____ , mortgagee, to declare a default and enforce the payment of all sums due

and payable on a certain mortgage executed and delivered to it by, _____ ,

mortgagor-seller, and duly recorded in the office of _____

for the County of _____ , State of _____ , in Book

_____ of Mortgages on page _____ , on the conveyance to the undersigned of the

premises on which such mortgage constitutes a first lien, does hereby assume and agree to pay

the obligation secured by said mortgage according to its terms and those of the note

accompanying it.

Date:

_____

AGREEMENT TO CONVERT SEPARATE PROPERTY INTO COMMUNITY PROPERTY

BE IT KNOWN, that for good consideration, the undersigned

_____ (Husband) and _____ (Wife) acknowledge that during

their marriage they acquired property, which by the laws of the State of _____ ,

is deemed community property. A list of said community property is annexed as Exhibit A.

Husband and Wife further acknowledge that any property they now hold individually is

annexed as Exhibit B and is hereby deemed to be community property.

Husband and Wife further agree that all after-acquired property, whether individually or

collectively held, shall also be deemed the community property of the parties.

This agreement shall be binding upon and inure to the benefit of the parties, their

successors, assigns and personal representatives.

Signed under seal this _____ day of _____ , 19 ____ .

_____
Husband

_____
Wife

STATE OF _____ }
COUNTY OF _____ }

On _____ before me, _____ , personally appeared
_____ , personally known to me (or
proved to me on the basis of satisfactory evidence) to be the person(s) whose name(s) is/are
subscribed to the within instrument and acknowledged to me that he/she/they executed the same
in his/her/their authorized capacity(ies), and that by his/her/their signature(s) on the instrument
the person(s), or the entity upon behalf of which the person(s) acted, executed the instrument.
WITNESS my hand and official seal.

Signature_____

Affiant _____Known _____Unknown
ID Produced_____
(Seal)

AGREEMENT TO EXTEND PERFORMANCE DATE

BE IT KNOWN, for good consideration,   of

(First Party), and   of

(Second Party), in and to a certain agreement

described as:

dated   , 19   (Agreement), do hereby acknowledge and agree that:

1.   Said Agreement provides that full performance on said agreement shall be completed on

or before   , 19   .

2.   That the parties acknowledge that said agreement cannot be performed and completed on

said date and that the parties hereupon desire to extend the performance date, as if said extended

date were the original date of performance.

3.   That the parties hereby mutually agree that the date for performance be continued and

extended to   , 19   , time being of the essence.

4.   There is no other change in terms or further extension allowed.

This agreement shall be binding upon and inure to the benefit of the parties, their

successors and assigns.

Signed this   day of   , 19   .

In the presence of:

_____   _____
Witness   First Party

_____   _____
Witness   Second Party

AGREEMENT TO EXTEND PERIOD OF OPTION

In consideration of the additional sum of

Dollars ($) paid to   , (hereinafter

"Seller"), by   , (hereinafter "Purchaser"), the period of that

certain option from Seller to Purchaser dated   , 19   , is hereby extended

to   o'clock   .m.,   19   .

The extension shall apply to all terms, provisions, and conditions, of the option and shall

be binding and inure to the Purchaser, his heirs, representatives, and assigns.

IN WITNESS WHEREOF, the parties have executed this instrument on   ,

19   .

Witnessed:

_____   _____

Witness   Seller

_____   _____

Witness   Purchaser

AGREEMENT TO LEASE

This agreement, made this   day of   , between

                (hereinafter "Lessor") and   (hereinafter "Lessee").

Lessor does hereby agree to grant, demise and let, and Lessee does hereby agree to take

                               , with appurtenances, from the   day of

to the   day of   , at the rent or sum of

        Dollars ($), to be paid as follows:

It is further agreed by and between the parties that the Lessor shall:

It is further agreed by and between the parties that the Lessee shall:

It is further agreed that the lease herein provided for shall be executed by the parties

hereto on the   day of   .

It is further agreed that in the event that the lease herein provided for shall be executed,

then and in such case the Lessor shall give, and the Lessee shall take, possession of said

premises on the   day of   , and the rent to be reserved in the said agreement

herein provided for shall commence and be payable from said last mentioned date.

It is further agreed that, in the event that either party hereto shall neglect, refuse or in any

way fail to execute the lease herein provided for, at said time and place, then the party in default

shall pay to the other party the sum of

Dollars ($) as liquidated damages and not as a penalty.

It is further agreed that the lease shall contain the following further provisions:

It is further agreed that these presents shall operate only as an agreement to lease, and not as a lease.

IN WITNESS WHEREOF, the parties hereto sign their names.

Witnessed:

_____   _____

Witness   Lessor

_____   _____

Witness   Lessee

AGREEMENT TO PURCHASE STOCK

For and in consideration of   Dollars ($),

                        , hereby agrees to sell, assign, transfer, and set over to

                        , his or her executors, representatives, and assigns, with full

power to transfer the same on the books of the corporation,   shares of the

stock of   , a corporation incorporated under the laws of State of

          , and having its principal place of business at

          . The stock is represented by the following certificates:

Seller warrants that the stock now stands in his or her name on the books of the

corporation and that all assessments to date are paid upon said shares.

agrees to purchase said shares for the consideration set forth above.

IN WITNESS WHEREOF, the parties have executed this stock purchase agreement on

          , 19   .

_____   _____

Buyer   Seller

AGREEMENT TO SELL PERSONAL PROPERTY

Purchase and Sales Agreement made by and between

of   (Seller), and

of   (Buyer).

Whereas, for good consideration the parties mutually agree that:

1.   Seller agrees to sell, and Buyer agrees to buy the following described property:

2.   Buyer agrees to pay to Seller and Seller agrees to accept as total purchase price the sum

of $, payable as follows:

$ deposit herewith paid

$ balance payable on delivery by cash,

bank or certified check

3.   Seller warrants it has good and legal title to said property, full authority to sell said property, and that said property shall be sold by warranty bill of sale free and clear of all liens, encumbrances, liabilities and adverse claims of every nature and description whatsoever.

4.   Said property is sold in "as is" condition, Seller disclaiming any warranty of merchantability, fitness or working order or condition of the property except that it shall be sold in its present condition, reasonable wear and tear excepted.

5.   The parties agree to transfer title on   , 19   , at the address of the Seller.

6.   This agreement shall be binding upon and inure to the benefit of the parties, their successors, assigns and personal representatives.

Signed this   day of   , 19   .

_____   _____
Witness   Buyer

_____   _____
Witness   Seller

AMENDMENT TO LEASE

BE IT KNOWN, that for good consideration

of _____ (Landlord), and _____ of

_____ (Tenant), under a certain lease agreement between them

for premises known as _____ , dated

_____ , 19 _____ , (Lease), hereby agree to modify and amend said Lease as to the

following terms:

All other Lease terms shall remain in force as contained in the original Lease, which

provisions are incorporated herein by reference.

This Lease Amendment shall become a part of the original Lease and shall be binding

upon and inure to the benefit of the parties, their successors, assigns and personal

representatives.

Signed under seal this _____ day of _____ , 19 _____ .

In the presence of:

_____   _____
Witness   Landlord

_____   _____
Witness   Tenant

ARBITRATION AGREEMENT

Agreement by and between   of   and

of   .

Be it acknowledged, that we the undersigned as our interests exist in and to a certain

contract, dispute, controversy, action or claim described as:

(claim) do hereby agree to resolve any dispute or controversy we now have or may ever have in

connection with or arising from said claim by binding Arbitration.

Said Arbitration shall be in accordance with the rules and procedures of the American

Arbitration for the City of   , which rules and procedures for arbitration are

incorporated herein by reference and the decision or award by the Arbitrators shall be final,

conclusive and binding upon each of us and enforceable in a court of law of proper jurisdiction.

All costs of arbitration shall be shared equally except that each party shall pay his own legal

costs.

Signed this   day of   , 19   .

In the presence of:

_____   _____

Witness   First Party

_____   _____

Witness   Second Party

ARTICLES OF INCORPORATION

We, the undersigned, as proper persons acting as incorporators of a corporation under the laws of the State of _____, adopt the following articles of incorporation:

FIRST   The name of the corporation is:_____.

SECOND   The period of its duration is:_____.

THIRD   The purpose of the corporation is:_____

_____.

FOURTH   The aggregate number of authorized shares is:_____.

FIFTH   The corporation will not commence business until at least_____

dollars have been received by it as consideration for the issuance of shares.

SIXTH   Cumulative voting of shares of stock [is], [is not] authorized.

SEVENTH   Provisions limiting or denying to shareholders the pre-emptive right to acquire

additional or treasury shares of the corporation are:_____

_____.

EIGHTH   Provisions for regulating the internal affairs of the corporation are:

_____.

NINTH   The address of the initial registered office of the corporation is:_____

_____ and the name

of its initial registered agent at such address is:_____.

TENTH   Address of the principal place of business is:_____

_____.

ELEVENTH The number of directors constituting the initial board of directors of the corporation is_____, and the names and address of the persons who are to serve as directors until the first annual meeting of shareholders or until their successors are elected and shall qualify are:

Name   Address

_____   _____

_____   _____

_____   _____

TWELFTH   The name and address of each incorporator is:

Name   Address

_____   _____

_____   _____

_____   _____

Date:

ASSIGNMENT BY ENDORSING ON LEASE

BE IT KNOWN, that for good and valuable consideration received, the undersigned Lessee hereby assigns all the Lessee's right, title, and interest in and to the within lease from and after _____, 19___, to _____, 19___, to _____, said premises to be used and occupied for _____ and no other purpose. We further agree that this assignment shall not release or relieve the undersigned, as original Lessee, from any liability under covenants of the lease.

Date: _____   _____

ASSIGNMENT OF ACCOUNTS RECEIVABLE
WITH NON-RECOURSE

FOR VALUE RECEIVED, the undersigned hereby assigns and transfers to

all rights, title and interest in and to the account(s)

receivable described as follows:

The undersigned warrants that the said account(s) are just and due and the undersigned has not received payment for same or any part thereof and has no knowledge of any dispute thereon; provided, however, that said account(s) are sold without recourse to the undersigned in the event of non-payment.

The undersigned further warrants that it has full title to said receivables, full authority to sell and transfer same, and that said receivables are sold free and clear of all liens, encumbrances or any known claims against said account(s).

This agreement shall be binding upon and inure to the benefit of the parties, their successors, assigns, and personal representatives.

Signed this   day of   , 19   .

_____

Signed in the presence of:

_____
Witness

ASSIGNMENT OF ACCOUNTS RECEIVABLE
WITH RECOURSE

FOR VALUE RECEIVED, the undersigned hereby assigns and transfers to

all right, title and interest in and to the account(s) receivable described as follows:

The undersigned warrants that said account(s) are just and due and the undersigned has not received payment for same or any part thereof.

It is further provided that if any said account does not make full payment within days, said account(s) will be re-purchased by the undersigned and the undersigned shall re-purchase same for the balance then owing on said account(s), the undersigned thereby guaranteeing collection of said receivables.

The undersigned further warrants that it has full title to said receivables, full authority to sell and transfer same, and that said receivables are sold free and clear of all liens, encumbrances or any known claims against said accounts.

This agreement shall be binding upon and inure to the benefit of the parties, their successors, assigns, and personal representatives.

Signed this   day of   , 19   .

_____

Signed in the presence of:

_____
Witness

ASSIGNMENT OF ASSETS

This agreement is made and entered into this   day of   , 19   ,
by and between   (Stockholder) and   ,
a Corporation hereinafter referred to as "Corporation."

WITNESSETH:

WHEREAS, on the   day of   , 19   , the Corporation was formed by Articles of Incorporation filed with the Secretary of State of   , and

WHEREAS, it is necessary to transfer certain assets into the Corporation in order to capitalize the Corporation; and

WHEREAS, Stockholder is desirous of transferring to the Corporation certain assets shown on the attached Exhibit "A," and the Corporation is desirous of acquiring said assets.

NOW, THEREFORE, for and in consideration of the mutual covenants and agreements hereinafter entered into, it is agreed as follows:

1.   Stockholder does hereby transfer and assign those assets listed on the attached Exhibit "A" to the Corporation.

2.   In consideration for said transfer the Corporation issues to Stockholder

(   ) shares of   stock in the Corporation, par value $ per share.

DATED this   day of   , 19   .

_____
Stockholder

By:_____
Corporation

ASSIGNMENT OF BANK ACCOUNT

BE IT KNOWN, that for consideration the undersigned,   ,

hereby sells, assigns, transfers and irrevocably sets over to   ,

Dollars ($) of the sums on deposit in

my name (Savings Account No.   ) in the

Bank, located at   , and further authorizes said

bank to pay over to   , assignee,

said sum out of the money on deposit in said bank account in the undersigned's name.

This assignment shall constitute notice to the

Bank of this assignment and direct authorization to such bank to act on this assignment.

IN WITNESS WHEREOF, the undersigned executed this assignment on   ,

19   .

Witnessed:

_____   _____
Witness   Seller

ASSIGNMENT OF CONTRACT

FOR VALUE RECEIVED, the undersigned Assignor hereby assigns, transfers and sets over to _____ (Assignee) all rights, title and interest held by the Assignor in and to the following described contract:

The Assignor warrants and represents that said contract is in full force and effect and is fully assignable.

The Assignee hereby assumes and agrees to perform all the remaining and executory obligations of the Assignor under the contract and agrees to indemnify and hold the Assignor harmless from any claim or demand resulting from non-performance by the Assignee.

The Assignee shall be entitled to all monies remaining to be paid under the contract, which rights are also assigned hereunder.

The Assignor warrants that the contract is without modification, and remains on the terms contained.

The Assignor further warrants that it has full right and authority to transfer said contract and that the contract rights herein transferred are free of lien, encumbrance or adverse claim.

This assignment shall be binding upon and inure to the benefit of the parties, their successors and assigns.

Signed this _____ day of _____ , 19___ .

_____
Assignor

_____
Assignee

ASSIGNMENT OF COPYRIGHT

FOR VALUE RECEIVED, the undersigned hereby sells, transfers and assigns unto
, and its successors, assigns, and personal representatives, all right, title and interest in and to the following described copyright and rights pertaining to said copyright, and to the works described as follows:

Title	Registration	Nature of Work

The undersigned warrants that it has good title to said copyright, that it is free of all liens, encumbrances or any known claims against said copyright, including infringement by or against said copyright.

This assignment shall be binding upon and inure to the benefit of the parties, their successors, assigns, and personal representatives.

Signed this   day of   , 19   .

In the presence of:

_____   _____
Witness   Assignor

ASSIGNMENT OF DAMAGE CLAIM

BE IT KNOWN, for value received, the undersigned hereby unconditionally and irrevocably assigns and transfers unto

(Assignee) and its successors, assigns and personal representatives, any and all claims, demands, and cause or causes of action of any kind whatsoever which the undersigned has or may have against   arising from the following:

The Assignee may in its own name, at its own expense, and for its own benefit prosecute said claim and collect, settle, compromise and grant releases on said claim as it in its sole discretion deems advisable, provided the undersigned shall reasonably assist and cooperate in the prosecution of said claim to the extent required or requested. Assignee shall be entitled to all judgments, awards and payments thereon.

The undersigned warrants it has full right and authority to assign this claim and that said claim is free and clear of any lien, encumbrance or other adverse interest. Assignor disclaims any representation as to the merits or collectibility of such claim.

This assignment shall be binding upon and inure to the benefit of the parties, their successors, assigns and personal representatives.

Signed this   day of   , 19   .

In the presence of:

_____   _____
Witness   Assignor

ASSIGNMENT OF INSURANCE POLICY

BE IT KNOWN, for value received, the undersigned

of   hereby irrevocably transfers

and assigns to   all legal and beneficial right, title and interest in

and to the within policy of insurance standing in my name and known as Policy No.

issued by the   Insurance Company. I also assign all cash

values, proceeds and benefits thereto arising, subject to the conditions of said policy and the

requirement of the issuing underwriter.

The undersigned warrants that it has full authority to transfer said policy, and shall

execute all further documents as may be required, by the underwriter.

This assignment shall be binding upon and inure to the benefit of the parties, their

successors, assigns and personal representatives.

Signed this   day of   , 19   .

In the presence of:

_____   _____

Witness   Name

                                                            _____

                                                            Address

                                                            _____

ASSIGNMENT OF LEASE

AGREEMENT by and between _____ (Tenant), and

_____ (Assignee), and _____ (Landlord).

For value received, it is agreed by and between the parties that:

1.   Tenant hereby agrees to assign, transfer and deliver to assignee all of Tenant's remaining rights in and to a certain lease between Tenant and Landlord for premises known as:

_____ ,

under lease dated _____ , 19 ____ .

2.   Assignee agrees to accept said Lease, pay all rents and punctually perform all of Tenant's remaining obligations under said Lease accruing after the date of delivery of possession to the assignee as contained herein. Assignee further agrees to indemnify and save harmless the Tenant from any breach of Assignee's obligations hereunder.

3.   The parties acknowledge that Tenant shall deliver possession of the leased premises to Assignee on _____ , 19 ____ (effective date); time being of the essence. All rights and other charges accrued under the Lease prior to said date shall be fully paid by Tenant, and thereafter by the Assignee.

4.   Landlord hereby assents to the assignment of lease, provided that:

      a) Assent to the assignment shall not discharge Tenant of its obligations to pay rent under the Lease in the event of breach by Assignee

      b) In the event of breach by Assignee, Landlord shall provide Tenant with written notice of same and Tenant shall have full rights to recover possession of the leased premises (in the name of Landlord, if necessary) and retain all rights for the duration of said Lease provided it shall pay all accrued rents and cure any other default.

5.   The parties acknowledge the lease to be in good standing and in full force and effect without modification.

6.   This agreement shall be binding upon and inure to the benefit of the parties, their successors, assigns and personal representatives.

Signed this   day of   , 19   .

In the presence of:

_____   _____
Witness   Tenant

_____   _____
Witness   Assignee

_____   _____
Witness   Landlord

ASSIGNMENT OF MONEY DUE

BE IT KNOWN, that for good and valuable consideration received, the undersigned,

, assigns, transfers, and sets over to

, assignee, all money now due and payable to me and to become due and

payable to the undersigned under a certain contract dated   , 19   , between the

undersigned and   , obligor, the subject matter of which

is

.

The undersigned hereby warrants that there has been no breach of the aforementioned

contract by any party, and that the undersigned is in full compliance with all the terms and

conditions of said contract, and has not assigned or encumbered all or any rights under said

contract.   .

The undersigned authorizes and directs   , obligor, to

deliver any and all checks, drafts, or payments to be issued pursuant to such contract to assignee;

and further authorizes assignee to receive such checks, drafts, or payments from obligor, and to

endorse my name on them and to collect any and all funds due or to become due pursuant

thereto.

IN WITNESS WHEREOF, the undersigned executed this assignment on   ,

19   .

_____

Assignor

ASSIGNMENT OF MORTGAGE

For and in consideration of   Dollars

($), the receipt of which is hereby acknowledged,

of   , hereby grants, assigns and transfers

to   , of   ,

that certain mortgage executed by   , dated   ,

19   , and recorded in the office of the   of

County, State of   , in Book   of Mortgage, at page   ,

together with the note described therein and the money to become due thereon with the interest

provided therein.

IN WITNESS WHEREOF, the undersigned has executed this assignment on   ,

19   .

_____

STATE OF   }
COUNTY OF
On   before me,   , personally appeared
                                         , personally known to me (or
proved to me on the basis of satisfactory evidence) to be the person(s) whose name(s) is/are
subscribed to the within instrument and acknowledged to me that he/she/they executed the same
in his/her/their authorized capacity(ies), and that by his/her/their signature(s) on the instrument
the person(s), or the entity upon behalf of which the person(s) acted, executed the instrument.
WITNESS my hand and official seal.

Signature_____

Affiant _____Known _____Unknown
ID Produced_____

(Seal)

ASSIGNMENT OF OPTION

In consideration of the payment to the undersigned of

Dollars ($), receipt which is hereby acknowledged, the undersigned hereby sells, transfers, assigns, and sets over the foregoing option and all my rights thereunder as purchaser, to

. By accepting this assignment the assignee undertakes and agrees to exercise the option pursuant to its terms.

Date:

_____

ASSIGNMENT OF TRADEMARK

The undersigned   of

(Owner) who registered in the United States Patent Office under registration number   ,

dated   , 19   ,   (Trademark), for good

consideration does hereby sell, transfer and convey all right, title and interest in said Trademark

and all rights and goodwill attaching thereto, unto

of   (Buyer).

The Owner warrants that said Trademark is in full force and good standing and there are

no other assignment of rights or licenses granted under said Trademark, or known infringements

by or against said Trademark.

Owner further warrants that he is the lawful Owner of said Trademark, that he has full

right and authority to transfer said Trademark and that said Trademark is transferred free and

clear of all liens, encumbrances and adverse claims.

This agreement shall be binding upon and inure to the benefit of the parties, their

successors, assigns and personal representatives.

Signed under seal this   day of   , 19   .

By: _____

STATE OF
COUNTY OF   }

On   before me,   , personally appeared
                                    , personally known to me (or
proved to me on the basis of satisfactory evidence) to be the person(s) whose name(s) is/are
subscribed to the within instrument and acknowledged to me that he/she/they executed the same
in his/her/their authorized capacity(ies), and that by his/her/their signature(s) on the instrument
the person(s), or the entity upon behalf of which the person(s) acted, executed the instrument.
WITNESS my hand and official seal.

Signature_____

Affiant   _____Known   _____Unknown
ID Produced_____
(Seal)

AUTHORIZATION TO RELEASE CONFIDENTIAL INFORMATION

Date:

To:

Dear

You are hereby authorized and requested to mail or deliver to:

_____
Name

_____
Address

_____

either original or copies of the below described documents or confidential information that you may have in your possession.

You may bill me for any costs associated with your compliance with this request and I thank you for your cooperation.

Very truly,

_____
Name

_____
Address

_____

AUTHORIZATION TO RELEASE CREDIT INFORMATION

Date:

To:

Please be advised I have a credit account with your firm and hereby request that a report of my credit history with you be forwarded to the below listed credit reporting agencies. You may consider this letter as my authorization to release this information.

Thank you for your cooperation.

_____

Signature

_____

Social Security Number

_____

Address

_____

_____

Signature of Joint Applicant (if any)

_____

Name of Account

_____

Account Number

Credit Reporting Agencies/Company

_____

Agency/Company

_____

Address

_____

_____

ATTN:

_____

Agency/Company

_____

Address

_____

_____

ATTN:

AUTHORIZATION TO RELEASE EMPLOYMENT INFORMATION

Date:

To:

      The undersigned   (Employee)
authorizes the release of the below checked employment information to:

_____ The following party:

_____ Any third party:

Those terms for which information may be released include: (Check)

_____ Salary
_____ Position and department
_____ Dates of employment
_____ Part-time/Full-time or hours worked
_____ Garnishes or wage attachments, if any
_____ Reason for separation
_____ Medical/accident/illness reports
_____ Work performance rating
_____ Other:

Thank you for your cooperation.

_____   _____
Employee Signature   Social Security Number

_____   _____
Address   Position or Title

_____   _____
Date of Employment   Position or Department

AUTHORIZATION TO RELEASE INFORMATION

From:

To:

    I have applied for a position with   .

    I have been requested to provide information for their use in reviewing my background and qualifications. Therefore, I hereby authorize the investigation of my past and present work, character, education, military and employment qualifications.

    The release in any manner of all information by you is hereby authorized whether such information is of record or not, and I do hereby release all persons, agencies, firms, companies, etc., from any damages resulting from providing such information.

    This authorization is valid for   days from date below. Please keep this copy of my release request for your files. Thank you.

Signature_____   Date_____

Witness_____   Date_____

AUTHORIZATION TO RELEASE MEDICAL INFORMATION

Date:

To:

Dear

     I hereby authorize and request that you release and deliver to:

_____

_____

_____

all my medical records, charts, files, prognoses, reports, x-rays, laboratory reports, clinical records, and such other information relative to my medical condition or my treatment at any time provided to me and all to the extent said information is available and within your possession. You may bill me for any costs. You are further requested not to disclose any information concerning my past or present medical condition to any other person without my express written permission.

     Thank you for your cooperation.

In the presence of:

_____   _____

Witness   Name

                                                     _____

                                                     Address

                                                     _____

AUTHORIZATION TO RETURN GOODS

Date:

To:

Please allow this letter to acknowledge that we shall accept certain return goods for credit. The terms for return are:

1.   The aggregate cost value of the goods subject to return shall not exceed $.

2.   We shall deduct   % of the cost price as handling charges to process the return goods, crediting your account.

3.   All return goods shall be in re-saleable condition and represent goods we either currently stock or can return to our supplier for credit. We reserve the right to reject non-conforming goods.

4.   Return goods must be invoiced and are subject to inspection and return approval before shipment to us.

5.   If goods are shipped via common carrier, you shall be responsible for all freight costs and risk of loss in transit. Goods shall not be considered accepted for return until we have received, inspected and approved said goods at our place of business.

6.   Our agreement to accept returns for credit is expressly conditional upon your agreement to pay any remaining balance due on the following terms:

You understand this return privilege is extended only to resolve your account balance and is not necessarily standing policy. Thank you for your cooperation in this matter.

Very truly,

_____

BAD CHECK NOTICE

Date:

To:

Dear

Payment on your Check No.   in the amount of $, tendered to us on   , 19   , has been dishonored by your bank. We have verified with your bank that there are still insufficient funds to pay the check.

Accordingly, we request that you replace this check with a cash (or certified check) payment.

Unless we receive good funds for said amount within   days, we shall immediately commence appropriate legal action to protect our interests. Upon receipt of replacement funds we shall return to you the dishonored check.

Very truly,

_____

Certified Mail, Return Receipt Requested

BALLOON NOTE

FOR VALUE RECEIVED, the undersigned promise to pay to the order of

the sum of

Dollars ($), with annual interest of   % on any unpaid balance.

This note shall be paid in   consecutive and equal installments of $ each with a first payment one   from date hereof, and the same amount on the same day of each   thereafter, provided the entire principal balance and any accrued but unpaid interest shall be fully paid on or before   , 19   . This note may be prepaid without penalty. All payments shall be first applied to interest and the balance to principal.

This note shall be due and payable upon demand of any holder hereof should the undersigned default in any payment beyond   days of its due date. All parties to this note waive presentment, demand and protest, and all notices thereto. In the event of default, the undersigned agree to pay all costs of collection and reasonable attorneys' fees. The undersigned shall be jointly and severally liable under this note.

Signed this   day of   , 19   .

Signed in the presence of:

_____   _____
Witness   Maker

_____   _____
Witness   Maker

BILL OF SALE

FOR VALUE RECEIVED, the undersigned

of   hereby sells and transfers unto

                                of   (Buyer),

and its successors and assigns forever, the following described goods and chattels:

Seller warrants and represents that it has good title to said property, full authority to sell and transfer same and that said goods and chattels are being sold free and clear of all liens, encumbrances, liabilities and adverse claims, of every nature and description.

Seller further warrants that it shall fully defend, protect, indemnify and save harmless the Buyer and its lawful successors and assigns from any and all adverse claim, that may be made by any party against said goods.

It is provided, however, that Seller disclaims any implied warranty of condition, merchantability or fitness for a particular purpose. Said goods being sold in their present condition "as is" and "where is."

Signed this   day of   , 19   .

In the presence of:

_____   _____
Witness   Seller's Signature

                                         _____
                                         Seller's Address

BREACH OF CONTRACT NOTICE

Date:

To:

Dear

    Reference is made to a certain agreement between us dated   , 19   , which agreement provides that:

    PLEASE TAKE NOTICE that you are in breach of your obligations under said contract in the following particulars:

    You are further advised that we shall hold you responsible for all actual and consequential damages arising from your breach.

                  Very truly,

_____

Name

_____

Address

_____

BULK SALES AFFIDAVIT

I, _____, the undersigned, being _____ (title) of _____ (Seller), of lawful age and first sworn, on oath state:

1.   The Undersigned executes this affidavit on behalf of the Seller under an intended bulk sale of inventory of a certain business known as _____, to _____ (Buyer).

2.   This affidavit is furnished pursuant to Article 6 of the Uniform Commercial Code, and is provided to the above named Buyer in connection with the sale described under said contract, and for purposes of providing creditors notice of said intended sale and transfer, pursuant to the Bulk Sales Act.

3.   That the attached is a true, complete and accurate list of all the creditors of Seller, which to the knowledge of the undersigned, assert or claim to assert one or more claims against the Seller, together with the correct business address of each such creditor or claimant and the amounts due and owing or otherwise claimed to be due as of this date.

Signed under seal this _____ day of _____, 19____.

_____
Seller's Representative

STATE OF _____ }
COUNTY OF _____

On _____ before me, _____, personally appeared _____, personally known to me (or proved to me on the basis of satisfactory evidence) to be the person(s) whose name(s) is/are subscribed to the within instrument and acknowledged to me that he/she/they executed the same in his/her/their authorized capacity(ies), and that by his/her/their signature(s) on the instrument the person(s), or the entity upon behalf of which the person(s) acted, executed the instrument. WITNESS my hand and official seal.

Signature_____

Affiant   _____Known   _____Unknown
ID Produced_____
                                                (Seal)

BULK SALES NOTICE

Date:

Notice to Creditors:

Please take notice that   , of   , (Seller) intends to make a bulk sale or transfer of its goods to   , (Buyer) whose address is or shall be:

To the knowledge of Buyer, the Seller has not done business under any other name during the past three years.

To the knowledge of Buyer, all debts of the Seller shall be paid in full as they fall due as part of this bulk sale.

Creditors are directed to send all bills and invoices to:

_____
Name

_____
Address

_____

The sale shall occur ten or more days from the date of receipt of this notice. This notice is provided in accordance with Article 6 (the Bulk Sales or Transfers Act, so-called), of the Uniform Commercial Code.

Very truly,

_____
Buyer

Registered Mail

CANCELLATION OF HOME SOLICITATION CONTRACT

Date:

To:

     You are hereby notified that the undersigned cancels the home solicitation contract dated

           , 19   , between   and   ,

for   .

     The undersigned has the right to cancel the contract for the reason that three business days have not elapsed from the date the undersigned executed the agreement.

     The undersigned hereby demands the return, within   days of the date hereof, sums heretofore paid in the amount of

$. On condition that payment is duly made to the undersigned, the undersigned shall, within   days of the date hereof, tender to seller at buyer's address the following:

                                      _____

CANCELLATION OF STOP-PAYMENT ORDER

Date:

To:

Dear

On   , 19   , we advised you to stop payment on the following

check:

        Check No:

        Dated:

        Amount:

        Maker:

        Payable to:

        Account No:

You may now honor and pay said check upon presentment since we cancel this previously issued stop-payment order.

_____

Account

_____

Account No.

By:_____

CERTIFICATE OF AMENDMENT

_____

, a corporation of the State of

, whose registered office is located at

, certifies pursuant to the provisions of state law, that at a meeting of the stockholders of said corporation called for the purpose of amending the articles of incorporation, and held on   , 19   , it was resolved by the vote of the holders of an appropriate majority of the shares of each class entitled to vote that ARTICLE   of the Articles of Incorporation is amended to read as follows:

ARTICLE

Signed on   , 19   .

By:_____
　　　　　　　　　　President

By:_____
　　　　　　　　　　Secretary

CERTIFICATE OF CORPORATE RESOLUTION

_____

I,   , Secretary of

, (Corporation) do hereby certify that at a duly constituted meeting of the Stockholders and Directors of the Corporation held at the office of the Corporation on , 19 , it was upon motion duly made and seconded, that it be VOTED:

It was upon further motion made and seconded that it be further VOTED: That in the capacity as of the Corporation is empowered, authorized and directed to execute, deliver and accept any and all documents and undertake all acts reasonably required or incidental to accomplish the foregoing vote, all on such terms and conditions as he in his discretion deems to be in the best interests of the Corporation.

I further certify that the foregoing votes are in full force this date without rescission, modification or amendment.

Signed this day of , 19 .

A TRUE RECORD

ATTEST

_____
Secretary/Clerk

(Corporate Seal)

CERTIFICATE OF LIMITED PARTNERSHIP

The partners of   , a limited partnership (hereinafter "partnership"), hereby execute the following certificate of limited partnership.

1. Name of the partnership. The name of the partnership shall be:

2. Name and address of registered agent for service of process. The registered agent for service of process shall be   . The registered office is located at:

3. Name and address of each general partner. The name(s) and address(es) of each general partner at the time of the original admission to the partnership of such partner are the following:

GENERAL PARTNER

BUSINESS, RESIDENCE OR
MAILING ADDRESS

4. There are at least two partners in the partnership, at least one of whom is a limited partner.

5. Effective Date. This partnership shall be deemed formed at the time of filing this certificate of Limited Partnership in the office of the secretary of State.

Signed: General Partner(s)

_____   Date:_____

_____   Date:_____

CERTIFICATE OF SALE OF BUSINESS UNDER AN ASSUMED NAME CERTIFICATE

The following is hereby certified:

1. The business that has been conducted at

under the   name of

, has been sold.

2. The names and residences of each person interested in the business, but now withdrawing from said business are:

3. Following are the names and addresses of the persons who will hereafter conduct the business:

4. The date when said person(s) withdrew from the business was   , 19   .

Dated:_____   _____

_____   _____

STATE OF
COUNTY OF   }

On   before me,   , personally appeared
                           , personally known to me (or proved to me on the basis of satisfactory evidence) to be the person(s) whose name(s) is/are subscribed to the within instrument and acknowledged to me that he/she/they executed the same in his/her/their authorized capacity(ies), and that by his/her/their signature(s) on the instrument the person(s), or the entity upon behalf of which the person(s) acted, executed the instrument. WITNESS my hand and official seal.

Signature_____

Affiant   _____Known   _____Unknown
ID Produced_____
(Seal)

CERTIFICATE OF TERMINATION OF BUSINESS
UNDER A FICTITIOUS OR ASSUMED NAME

CERTIFICATE

The following is hereby certified:

1. Pursuant to state law, a certificate to conduct business under the

name of _____ at _____ ,

was filed in the office of the _____ on _____ , 19 ,

by _____ and _____ .

2. The filing of such certificate is no longer required for the following reason:

3. The undersigned constitute majority of the persons named in the original or in the

most recent amended certificate as conducting business under the _____ name

of _____ at

.

Dated:_____   _____

_____   _____

STATE OF _____ }
COUNTY OF _____ }

On _____ before me, _____ , personally appeared
_____ , personally known to me (or
proved to me on the basis of satisfactory evidence) to be the person(s) whose name(s) is/are
subscribed to the within instrument and acknowledged to me that he/she/they executed the same
in his/her/their authorized capacity(ies), and that by his/her/their signature(s) on the instrument
the person(s), or the entity upon behalf of which the person(s) acted, executed the instrument.
WITNESS my hand and official seal.

Signature_____

Affiant _____Known _____Unknown
ID Produced_____
(Seal)

CERTIFICATE OF WITHDRAWAL OF PARTNER FROM BUSINESS UNDER A FICTITIOUS OR ASSUMED NAME

CERTIFICATE

The following is hereby certified:

1. The undersigned, _____ , and whose address is _____ , have withdrawn as _____ partner(s) from the partnership doing business under the _____ name of

_____ .

2. The partnership has its principal place of business located at:

3. The _____ name certificate with respect to said business name was filed on

_____ , 19 ____ , in the office of _____ , State

of _____ .

Dated:_____   _____

_____   _____

STATE OF _____
COUNTY OF _____   }

On _____ before me, _____ , personally appeared _____ , personally known to me (or proved to me on the basis of satisfactory evidence) to be the person(s) whose name(s) is/are subscribed to the within instrument and acknowledged to me that he/she/they executed the same in his/her/their authorized capacity(ies), and that by his/her/their signature(s) on the instrument the person(s), or the entity upon behalf of which the person(s) acted, executed the instrument. WITNESS my hand and official seal.

Signature_____

Affiant   _____Known   _____Unknown
ID Produced_____
(Seal)

CHANGE OF BENEFICIARY

Date:

To:

       Notice is hereby given to you to change the beneficiary on

Policy No.   , of   .

The policy was issued by

(hereinafter "company"). Subject to the provisions attached and marked as Exhibit A, the

beneficiary is to be changed from   of

                                          to

of   .

       This request for change of beneficiary shall take effect as of the day it is signed,

accepted, and recorded at the home office of the company. Any previous selection of a

beneficiary is hereby revoked.

                                            _____

CHANGE OF BENEFICIARY NOTICE

Date:

To:

Dear

      BE IT ACKNOWLEDGED, that   of   ,

is hereby designated beneficiary in and to a certain life insurance policy numbered

and issued by   . Said policy is dated   , 19   , the

present death benefit payable is in the amount of $ on the life of the undersigned.

This change of beneficiary acknowledgement terminates all prior designations of beneficiary

heretofore made. Please forward any necessary change of beneficiary forms.

      Signed under seal this   day of   , 19   .

_____

Insured

_____

Address

_____

STATE OF

COUNTY OF   }

On   before me,   , personally appeared

           , personally known to me (or

proved to me on the basis of satisfactory evidence) to be the person(s) whose name(s) is/are
subscribed to the within instrument and acknowledged to me that he/she/they executed the same
in his/her/their authorized capacity(ies), and that by his/her/their signature(s) on the instrument
the person(s), or the entity upon behalf of which the person(s) acted, executed the instrument.
WITNESS my hand and official seal.

Signature_____

           Affiant   _____Known   _____Unknown
           ID Produced_____

                          (Seal)

CHANGE OF LOSS PAYEE NOTICE

Date:

To:

     PLEASE BE ADVISED, that   , is hereby

designated loss payee in and to a certain casualty insurance policy numbered   ,

issued by   , said policy dated   , 19   ,

wherein the undersigned is named insured. This change of loss payee acknowledgement

terminates all prior designations of loss payee heretofore made, and you are to delete said

former party as the loss payee.

     Signed under seal this   day of   , 19   .

_____

STATE OF   }
COUNTY OF

On   before me,   , personally appeared
           , personally known to me (or
proved to me on the basis of satisfactory evidence) to be the person(s) whose name(s) is/are
subscribed to the within instrument and acknowledged to me that he/she/they executed the same
in his/her/their authorized capacity(ies), and that by his/her/their signature(s) on the instrument
the person(s), or the entity upon behalf of which the person(s) acted, executed the instrument.
WITNESS my hand and official seal.

Signature_____

                Affiant   _____Known   _____Unknown
                ID Produced_____
                                       (Seal)

CHANGE WORK ORDER

Hirer:

Contractor:

Contract Date:

    1. The Hirer authorizes and the Contractor agrees to make the following work changes to the above dated contract:

    2. The agreed additional charge for the above change is

                Dollars ($).

Dated:

_____   _____
Hirer   Contractor

CHECK STOP-PAYMENT

Date:

To:

Dear

       Please be advised that you are hereby directed to place a stop-payment order and refuse payment against our account upon presentment of the following check:

          Name of payee:

          Date of Check:

          Check Number:

          Amount:

       This stop-payment order shall remain in effect until further written notice.

       Please advise if this check has been previously paid, and the date of payment.

       Thank you for your cooperation.

_____

Name of Account

_____

Account Number

By:_____

CHILD GUARDIANSHIP CONSENT FORM

The undersigned   , of

                , State of   , hereby appoint

                , of   ,

State of   , as the legal guardian of the person of our child(ren). Said guardian shall have the following powers:

Executed this   day of   , 19   .

_____

_____

CLAIM OF LIEN

STATE OF   }
COUNTY OF   }

        BEFORE ME, the undersigned Notary Public, personally appeared_____
_____ who duly sworn says that he is (the lienor herein) (the agent of the lienor herein) whose address is _____ and that in accordance with a contract with _____lienor furnished labor, services or materials consisting of:_____ on the following described real property in_____County, State of_____, described as_____ _____and owned by_____ of a total value of_____ dollars ($_____) of which there remains unpaid $_____, and furnished the first of the items on _____, 19_____ , by _____and, (if required) that the lienor served copies of the notice on the contractor on _____, 19___, by_____, and on the subcontractor _____ on_____, 19___, by _____.

                               _____
                               Lienor

                   By:_____
                            Agent

On   before me,   , personally appeared , personally known to me (or proved to me on the basis of satisfactory evidence) to be the person(s) whose name(s) is/are subscribed to the within instrument and acknowledged to me that he/she/they executed the same in his/her/their authorized capacity(ies), and that by his/her/their signature(s) on the instrument the person(s), or the entity upon behalf of which the person(s) acted, executed the instrument. WITNESS my hand and official seal.

Signature_____   Affiant   _____Known   _____Unknown
                                             ID Produced _____
                                                            (Seal)

CODICIL

I, _____, a resident of the County of _____,
State of _____, declare that this is the _____ codicil to my last
will and testament, which is dated _____, 19____.

I add or change said last will in the following manner:

Otherwise, I hereby confirm and republish my will dated _____, 19____, in all
respects other than those herein mentioned.

I subscribe my name to this codicil this _____ day of _____, 19____,
at _____, in the presence of _____ and
_____, attesting witnesses, who subscribe their names hereto at
my request and in my presence.

_____

Testator's Signature

ATTESTATION CLAUSE

On the date last above written, _____, known to us
to be the person whose signature appears at the end of this codicil, declared to us, the
undersigned, that the foregoing instrument, consisting, of _____ pages was the

codicil to will dated _____ , 19 ___ , then signed the codicil in our presence, and at

request, in the presence of each other, we now sign our names as witnesses.

_____   residing at _____

Witness

                                                        _____

_____   residing at _____

Witness

                                                        _____

_____   residing at _____

Witness

                                                        _____

State of
County of   }

We, _____ , _____ ,

_____ , and _____ ,
the testator and the witnesses, respectively, whose names are signed to the attached and foregoing instrument, were sworn and
declared to the undersigned that the testator signed the instrument as his/her codicil and that each of the witnesses, in the
presence of the testator and each other, signed the codicil as a witness.

Testator: _____   Witness _____

                                                 Witness _____

                                                 Witness _____

On _____ before me, _____ ,
appeared
personally known to me (or proved to me on the basis of satisfactory evidence) to be the person(s) whose name(s) is/are
subscribed to the within instrument and acknowledged to me that he/she/they executed the same in his/her/their authorized
capacity(ies), and that by his/her/their signature(s) on the instrument the person(s), or the entity upon behalf of which the
person(s) acted, executed the instrument.
WITNESS my hand and official seal.

Signature_____

                                        Affiant _____ Known_____Produced ID
                                        Type of ID_____
                                                               (Seal)

COHABITATION AGREEMENT

BE IT KNOWN, this agreement is made this   day of   , 19   ,

by   and

who presently reside in the State of   .

1.   Relationship: The parties wish to live together in a relationship similar to matrimony but do not wish to be bound by the statutory or common-law provisions relating to marriage.

2.   Duration of Relationship: It is agreed that we will live together for an indefinite period of time subject to the following terms:

3.   Property: Any real or personal property acquired by us or either of us during the relationship shall be considered to be our separate property. All property listed on the pages attached is made a part of this agreement by this reference. The property now and hereinafter belongs to the party under whose name it is listed prior to the making of this agreement. All listed property is and shall continue to be the separate property of the person who now owns it. All property received by either of us by gift or inheritance during our relationship shall be the separate property of the one who receives it.

4.   Income: All income of either of us and all our accumulations during the existence of our relationship shall be maintained in one fund. Our debts and expenses arising during the existence of our union shall be paid out of this fund. Each of us shall have an equal interest in this sum, and equal right to its management and control, and be equally entitled to the surplus remaining after payment of all debts and expenses.

5.   Termination: Our relationship may be terminated at the sole will and decision of either of us, expressed by a written notice given to the other.

6.   Modification of this Agreement: This agreement may be modified by an agreement in writing by both parties, with the exception that no modifications may decrease the obligations

that may be imposed regarding any children born of our union.

7.   Application of Law: The validity of this agreement shall be determined solely under the laws of the State of   as they may from time to time be changed.

8.   Neither party shall maintain any action or claim as against the other for support, alimony, compensation or for rights to any property existing prior to this date, or acquired during or subsequent to the date of termination.

9.   The parties enter into this agreement of their own will and accord without reliance on any other inducement or promise.

10.   Each party to this agreement has had the opportunity to have this agreement reviewed by independent counsel.

      Signed this   day of   , 19   .

_____

First Party

_____

Second Party

COMMERCIAL LEASE

This lease is made between   , herein called Lessor, and
                    , herein called Lessee.
Lessee hereby offers to lease from Lessor the premises situated in the City of
         , County of   , State of   , described as

                    , upon the following TERMS and CONDITIONS:

1.   **Term and Rent.** Lessor demises the above premises for a term of   years, commencing   , 19   , and terminating on   , 19   , or sooner as provided herein at the annual rental of   Dollars ($) payable in equal installments in advance on the first day of each month for that month's rental, during the term of this lease. All rental payments shall be made to Lessor, at the address specified above.

2.   **Use.** Lessee shall use and occupy the premises for   .
The premises shall be used for no other purpose. Lessor represents that the premises may lawfully be used for such purpose.

3.   **Care and Maintenance of Premises.** Lessee acknowledges that the premises are in good order and repair, unless otherwise indicated herein. Lessee shall, at his own expense and at all times, maintain the premises in good and safe condition, including plate glass, electrical wiring, plumbing and heating installations and any other system or equipment upon the premises, and shall surrender the same at termination hereof, in as good condition as received, normal wear and tear excepted. Lessee shall be responsible for all repairs required, excepting the roof, exterior walls, structural foundations, and:

4.   **Alterations.** Lessee shall not, without first obtaining the written consent of Lessor, make any alterations, additions, or improvements, in, to or about the premises.

5.   **Ordinances and Statutes.** Lessee shall comply with all statutes, ordinances and requirements of all municipal, state and federal authorities now in force, or which may hereafter be in force, pertaining to the premises, occasioned by or affecting the use thereof by Lessee.

6.   **Assignment and Subletting.** Lessee shall not assign this lease or sublet any portion of the premises without prior written consent of the Lessor, which shall not be unreasonably withheld. Any such assignment or subletting without consent shall be void and, at the option of the Lessor, may terminate this lease.

7.   **Utilities.** All applications and connections for necessary utility services on the demised premises shall be made in the name of Lessee only, and Lessee shall be solely liable for utility charges as they become due, including those for sewer, water, gas, electricity, and telephone services.

8.   Entry and Inspection. Lessee shall permit Lessor or Lessor's agents to enter upon the premises at reasonable times and upon reasonable notice, for the purpose of inspecting the same, and will permit Lessor at any time within sixty (60) days prior to the expiration of this lease, to place upon the premises any usual "To Let" or "For Lease" signs, and permit persons desiring to lease the same to inspect the premises thereafter.

9.   Possession. If Lessor is unable to deliver possession of the premises at the commencement hereof, Lessor shall not be liable for any damage caused thereby, nor shall this lease be void or voidable, but Lessee shall not be liable for any rent until possession is delivered. Lessee may terminate this lease if possession is not delivered within   days of the commencement of the term hereof.

10.   Indemnification of Lessor. Lessor shall not be liable for any damage or injury to Lessee, or any other person, or to any property, occurring on the demised premises or any part thereof, and Lessee agrees to hold Lessor harmless from any claim for damages, no matter how caused.

11.   Insurance. Lessee, at his expense, shall maintain plate glass and public liability insurance including bodily injury and property damage insuring Lessee and Lessor with minimum coverage as follows:

Lessee shall provide Lessor with a Certificate of Insurance showing Lessor as additional insured. The Certificate shall provide for a ten-day written notice to Lessor in the event of cancellation or material change of coverage. To the maximum extent permitted by insurance policies which may be owned by Lessor or Lessee, Lessee and Lessor, for the benefit of each other, waive any and all rights of subrogation which might otherwise exist.

12.   Eminent Domain. If the premises or any part thereof or any estate therein, or any other part of the building materially affecting Lessee's use of the premise, shall be taken by eminent domain, this lease shall terminate on the date when title vests pursuant to such taking. The rent, and any additional rent, shall be apportioned as of the termination date, and any rent paid for any period beyond that date shall be repaid to Lessee. Lessee shall not be entitled to any part of the award for such taking or any payment in lieu thereof, but Lessee may file a claim for any taking of fixtures and improvements owned by Lessee, and for moving expenses.

13.   Destruction of Premises. In the event of a partial destruction of the premises during the term hereof, from any cause, Lessor shall forthwith repair the same, provided that such repairs can be made within sixty (60) days under existing governmental laws and regulations, but such partial destruction shall not terminate this lease, except that Lessee shall be entitled to a proportionate reduction of rent while such repairs are being made, based upon the extent to which the making of such repairs shall interfere with the business of Lessee on the premises. If such repairs cannot be made within said sixty (60) days, Lessor, at his option, may make the same within a reasonable time, this lease continuing in effect with the rent proportionately abated as aforesaid, and in the event that Lessor shall not elect to make such repairs which cannot be made within sixty (60) days, this lease may be terminated at the option of either party. In the event that the building in which the demised premises may be situated is destroyed to an extent of not less than one-third of the replacement costs thereof, Lessor may elect to terminate

this lease whether the demised premises be injured or not. A total destruction of the building in which the premises may be situated shall terminate this lease.

14.   Lessor's Remedies on Default. If Lessee defaults in the payment of rent, or any additional rent, or defaults in the performance of any of the other covenants or conditions hereof, Lessor may give Lessee notice of such default and if Lessee does not cure any such default within   days, after the giving of such notice (or if such other default is of such nature that it cannot be completely cured within such period, if Lessee does not commence such curing within such   days and thereafter proceed with reasonable diligence and in good faith to cure such default), then Lessor may terminate this lease on not less than   days' notice to Lessee. On the date specified in such notice the term of this lease shall terminate, and Lessee shall then quit and surrender the premises to Lessor, but Lessee shall remain liable as hereinafter provided. If this lease shall have been so terminated by Lessor, Lessor may at any time thereafter resume possession of the premises by any lawful means and remove Lessee or other occupants and their effects. No failure to enforce any term shall be deemed a waiver.

15.   Security Deposit. Lessee shall deposit with Lessor on the signing of this lease the sum of

Dollars ($) as security deposit for the performance of Lessee's obligations under this lease, including without limitation the surrender of possession of the premises to Lessor as herein provided. If Lessor applies any part of the deposit to cure any default of Lessee, Lessee shall on demand deposit with Lessor the amount so applied so that Lessor shall have the full deposit on hand at all times during the term of this lease.

16.   Tax Increase. In the event there is any increase during any year of the term of this lease in the City, County or State real estate taxes over and above the amount of such taxes assessed for the tax year during which the term of this lease commences, whether because of increased rate or valuation, Lessee shall pay to Lesser upon presentation of paid tax bills an amount equal to   % of the increase in taxes upon the land and building in which the leased premises are situated. In the event that such taxes are assessed for a tax year extending beyond the term of the lease, the obligation of Lessee shall be proportionate to the portion of the lease term included in such year.

17.   Common Area Expenses. In the event the demised premises are situated in a shopping center or in a commercial building in which there are common areas, Lessee agrees to pay his pro-rata share of maintenance, taxes, and insurance for the common area.

18.   Attorney's Fees. In case suit should be brought for recovery of the premises, or for any sum due hereunder, or because of any act which may arise out of the possession of the premises, by either party, the prevailing party shall be entitled to all costs incurred in connection with such action, including a reasonable attorney's fee.

19.   Notices. Any notice which either party may, or is required to give, shall be given by mailing the same, postage prepaid, to Lessee at the premises, or Lessor at the address first written, or at such other places as may be designated by the parties from time to time.

20.   Heirs, Assigns, Successors. This lease is binding upon and inures to the benefit of the heirs, assigns and successors in interest to the parties.

21.   Option to Renew. Provided that Lessee is not in default in the performance of this lease, Lessee shall have the option to renew the lease for an additional term of   months commencing at the expiration of the initial lease term. All of the terms and conditions of the lease shall apply during the renewal term except that the monthly rent shall be the sum of $. The option shall be exercised by written notice given to Lessor not less than   days prior to the expiration of the initial lease term. If notice is not given in the manner provided herein within the time specified, this option shall expire.

22.   Subordination. This lease is and shall be subordinated to all existing and future liens and encumbrances against the property.

23.   Entire Agreement. The foregoing constitutes the entire agreement between the parties and may be modified only by a writing signed by both parties. The following Exhibits, if any, have been made a part of this lease before the parties' execution hereof:

        Signed this   day of   , 19   .

_____   _____

By: _____   By: _____
        Lessee   Lessor

CONDITIONAL SALE AGREEMENT

The undersigned Purchaser hereby purchases from

_____

_____

(Seller)

the following goods:

Sales price	$_____
Sales tax (if any)	$_____
Finance charge	$_____
Insurance (if any)	$_____
Other charges (if any)	$_____
Total purchase price	$_____
Less:	$_____

Down Payment $_____

Other credits $_____

Total Credits	$_____
Amount financed	$_____

ANNUAL INTEREST RATE_____%

The amount financed shall be payable in   installments of $
each, commencing   from date hereof.

Seller shall retain title to goods until payment of the full purchase price, subject to allocation of payments and release of security interest as required by law. The undersigned agrees to safely keep the goods, free from other liens and encumbrances at the below address, and not remove goods without consent of Seller.

Purchaser agrees to execute all financing statements as may be required of Seller to perfect this conditional sales agreement.

At the election of Seller, the Purchaser shall keep goods adequately insured, naming Seller loss-payee.

The full balance shall become due on default; with the undersigned paying all reasonable attorneys fees and costs of collection. Upon default, Seller shall have the right to retake the goods, hold and dispose of same and collect expenses, together with any deficiency due from Purchaser, but subject to the Purchaser's right to redeem pursuant to law and the Uniform Commercial Code.

THIS IS A CONDITIONAL SALE AGREEMENT.

Accepted:

_____   _____
Seller   Purchaser

                                   _____
                                   Address

                                   By:_____

CONDUCT OF BUSINESS UNDER FICTITIOUS OR ASSUMED NAME

Date:

To:

State of:

Pursuant to   , relating to the conduct of business under

name, the undersigned,

hereby present(s) for filing the following application in the office of:

1. The   name under which the business is, or will be, carried on is:

2. The real name and address of each person owning or interested in the business is:

3. The nature of the business is:

4. The business will be conducted at:

_____

_____

STATE OF

COUNTY OF   }

On   before me,   , personally appeared
                              , personally known to me (or
proved to me on the basis of satisfactory evidence) to be the person(s) whose name(s) is/are
subscribed to the within instrument and acknowledged to me that he/she/they executed the same
in his/her/their authorized capacity(ies), and that by his/her/their signature(s) on the instrument
the person(s), or the entity upon behalf of which the person(s) acted, executed the instrument.
WITNESS my hand and official seal.

Signature_____

Affiant   _____Known   _____Unknown
ID Produced_____
(Seal)

CONFIDENTIALITY AGREEMENT

AGREEMENT and acknowledgement between   (Company)
and   (Undersigned).

Whereas, the Company agrees to furnish the Undersigned access to certain confidential information relating to the affairs of the Company solely for purposes of:

Whereas, the Undersigned agrees to review, examine, inspect or obtain such information only for the purposes described above, and to otherwise hold such information confidential and secret pursuant to the terms of this agreement.

BE IT KNOWN, that the Company has or shall furnish to the Undersigned certain confidential information, described on attached list, and may further allow suppliers, customers, employees or representatives of the Company to disclose information to the Undersigned, all on the following conditions:

1.   The Undersigned agrees to hold all confidential or proprietary information or trade secrets ("information") in trust and confidence and agrees that it shall be used only for the contemplated purpose, and shall not be used for any other purpose or disclosed to any third party under any circumstances whatsoever.

2.   No copies may be made or retained of any written information supplied.

3.   At the conclusion of our discussions, or upon demand by the Company, all information, including written notes, photographs, or memoranda shall be promptly returned to the Company. Undersigned shall retain no copies or written documentation relating thereto.

4.   This information shall not be disclosed to any employee, consultant or third party unless said party agrees to execute and be bound by the terms of this agreement, and disclosure by Company is first approved.

5.   It is understood that the Undersigned shall have no obligation with respect to any

information known by the Undersigned or as may be generally known within the industry prior to date of this agreement, or that shall become common knowledge within the industry thereafter.

6.   The Undersigned acknowledges the information disclosed herein is proprietary or trade secrets and in the event of any breach, the Company shall be entitled to injunctive relief as a cumulative and not necessarily successive or exclusive remedy to a claim for monetary damages.

7.   This agreement shall be binding upon and inure to the benefit of the parties, their successors and assigns.

8.   This constitutes the entire agreement.

        Signed this   day of   , 19   .

Witnessed:

_____   _____
Witness   First Party

_____   _____
Witness   Second Party

CONFIRMATION OF VERBAL ORDER

Date:

To:

Dear

This letter shall confirm your acceptance of our verbal order of   , 19   .

A copy of our confirmatory purchase order containing the stated terms is enclosed as Purchase Order No.:

Unless we receive written objection within ten (10) days of your receipt of this order, we shall consider the order confirmed on its terms and shall anticipate delivery of all ordered goods on the date indicated.

Thank you for your cooperation.

Very truly,

_____

CONSENT FOR DRUG/ALCOHOL SCREEN TESTING

If you are offered and accept employment with
(company), in the interest of safety for all concerned, you will be required to take a urine test for drug and/or alcohol use.

I, , have been fully informed of the reason for this urine test for drug and/or alcohol (I understand what I am being tested for), the procedure involved, and do hereby freely give my consent. In addition, I understand that the results of this test will be forwarded to my potential employer and become part of my record.

If this test is positive, and for this reason I am not hired, I understand that I will be given the opportunity to explain the results of this test.

I hereby authorize these test results to be released to
(company name).

Signature_____ Date_____

Witness_____ Date_____

CONSENT TO ASSIGNMENT

The undersigned,   , as   under a certain contract dated   , 19   , executed at   , hereby consents to the assignment of the rights and obligations of   as   under said contract to   , assignee.

Date:

_____

CONSENT TO PARTIAL ASSIGNMENT

The undersigned, _____, hereby consents to the assignment by _____, assignor, of the sum of _____ dollars ($_____), which constitutes a portion of the amount due from me to him or her on completion of the performance of his or her obligation under a certain contract for _____, between myself and _____, assignor, to _____, assignee.

Date: _____   _____

CONSIGNMENT AGREEMENT

Agreement made this   day of   , 19   , by and between

(Consignor) and

(Customer).

1.   Customer acknowledges receipt of goods as described on annexed schedule. Said goods shall remain property of Consignor until sold. Consignor may from time to time ship additional consigned goods as ordered.

2.   The Customer at its own cost and expense agrees to keep and display the goods only in its place of business, and agrees, on demand made before any sale, to return the same in good order and condition. Customer may at its own election return goods to Consignor.

3.   The Customer agrees to use its best efforts to sell the goods for the Consignor's account on cash terms, and at such prices as shall from time to time be set by Consignor, and at no lesser price.

4.   The Customer agrees, upon sale, to maintain proceeds due Consignor in trust, and separate and apart from its own funds and deliver such proceeds, less commission, to Consignor together with an accounting within   days of said sale.

5.   The Customer agrees to accept as full payment a commission equal to   % of the gross sales price (exclusive of any sales tax), which the Customer shall collect and remit.

6.   The Customer agrees to permit the Consignor to enter the premises at reasonable times to examine and inspect the goods, and reconcile an accounting of sums due.

7.   Customer acknowledges that title to the goods shall remain with Consignor until goods are sold in the ordinary course of business.

8.   Risk of loss of the goods shall be the responsibility of Customer while said goods are within its possession.

9.   This agreement may be terminated by either party at will. Upon termination all unsold goods shall be returned together with payment of any monies due.

10.   This agreement is not assignable and shall not be modified except by written modification.

11.   This agreement shall be binding upon and inure to the benefit of the parties, their successors, assigns and personal representatives.

_____   _____
Consignor   Customer

Record in public filing office

CONSULTING SERVICES AGREEMENT

The parties to this agreement are the following:

Consultant:

Client:

The consultant will consult with and advise in the following matters:

FEES & EXPENSES:

The consultant's fee for the above services is $

based upon an estimated duration of   .

A retainer of $ is immediately due and payable. Future payments will be

made upon completion of this assignment, or in exchange for the documents provided.

Expenses will be reimbursed upon receipt of the invoice.

Signed this   day of   , 19   .

_____   _____
Consultant   Client

CONSUMER LOAN AGREEMENT

1.   Parties: The undersigned is   , the Borrower, and the Lender is   .

2.   Date of Agreement:

3.   Promise to Pay: Within   months from today, I promise to pay to lender   dollars ($), and interest and other charges stated below.

4.   Responsibility: Although this agreement may be signed below by more than one person, I understand that we are each as individuals responsible for paying back the full amount.

5.   Breakdown of Loan: This is what I will pay:

     1. Amount of Loan: $_____

     2. Other (Describe): $_____

     3. Amount financed: $_____

        (Add 1 and 2)

     4. Finance charge: $_____

     5. Total of payments: $_____

        (Add 3 and 4)

     ANNUAL PERCENTAGE RATE_____%

6.   Repayment: This is how I will repay: I will repay the amount of this note in   equal uninterrupted monthly installments of $ each on the   day of each month starting on the   day of   , 19   , and ending on   , 19   .

7.   Prepayment: I have the right to prepay the whole outstanding amount at any time. If I do, or if this loan is refinanced—that is, replaced by a new note—you will refund the unearned finance charge, figured by the Rule of 78—a commonly used formula for figuring rebates on installment loans.

8.   Late Charge: Any installment not paid within ten (10) days of its due date shall be subject to a late charge of 5% of the payment, not to exceed $ for any such late installment.

9.   Security: To protect lender, I give what is known as a security interest or mortgage in:(Describe)

10.   Default: If for any reason I fail to make any payment on time, I shall be in default. The lender can then demand immediate payment of the entire remaining unpaid balance of this loan, without giving anyone further notice. If I have not paid the full amount of the loan when the final payment is due, the lender will charge me interest on the unpaid balance at

percent (%) per year.

11.   Right of Offset: If this loan becomes past due, the lender will have the right to pay this loan from any deposit or security I have with this lender without notice to me.   If the lender gives me an extension of time to pay this loan, I still must repay the entire loan.

12.   Collection fees: If this note is placed with an attorney for collection, then I agree to pay an attorney's fee of fifteen percent (15%) of the unpaid balance. This fee will be added to the unpaid balance of the loan.

13.   Co-borrowers: If I am signing this agreement as a co-borrower, I agree to be equally responsible with the borrower for this loan.

Agreed To:

_____   _____
Borrower   Lender

_____
Borrower

CONTRACT

Agreement made this   day of   , 19   , between   ,

hereinafter   , and   , hereinafter   .

The parties to this agreement, in consideration of the mutual covenants and stipulations set out, agree as follows:

SECTION

INSTRUMENT AS ENTIRE AGREEMENT

This instrument contains the entire agreement between the parties, and no statements, promises, or inducements made by either party or agent of either party that are not contained in this contract shall be valid or binding; this contract may not be enlarged, modified, or altered except in writing signed by both parties and endorsed on this agreement.

SECTION

EFFECT OF AGREEMENT

This agreement shall inure to the benefit of and be binding on the heirs, executors, assignees, and successors of the respective parties.

IN WITNESS WHEREOF, the parties have executed this agreement on the day and year first above written.

_____   _____

First Party   Second Party

CONTRACTOR AGREEMENT

THIS AGREEMENT made the   day of   , 19   by
and between   , hereinafter called the Contractor
and   , hereinafter called the Owner.

WITNESSETH, that the Contractor and the Owner for the considerations named agree as
follows:

ARTICLE 1.   SCOPE OF THE WORK
The Contractor shall furnish all of the materials and perform all of the work shown on the
drawings and/or described in the specifications entitled Exhibit A, as annexed hereto as it pertains
to work to be performed on property at:

ARTICLE 2.   TIME OF COMPLETION
The work to be performed under this Contract shall be commenced on or before   ,
19   and shall be substantially completed on or before   , 19   . Time is of the
essence. The following constitutes substantial commencement of work pursuant to this proposal and
contract: (Specify)

ARTICLE 3.   THE CONTRACT PRICE
The Owner shall pay the Contractor for the material and labor to be performed under the
Contract the sum of   Dollars ($), subject to
additions and deductions pursuant to authorized change orders.

ARTICLE 4.   PROGRESS PAYMENTS
Payments of the Contract Price shall be paid in the manner following:

ARTICLE 5.   GENERAL PROVISIONS
1. All work shall be completed in a workman-like manner and in compliance with all
building codes and other applicable laws.
2. The contractor shall furnish a plan and scale drawing showing the shape, size
dimensions, and construction and equipment specifications for home improvements, a description
of the work to be done and description of the materials to be used and the equipment to be used
or installed, and the agreed consideration for the work.
3. To the extent required by law all work shall be performed by individuals duly licensed and
authorized by law to perform said work.
4. Contractor may at its discretion engage subcontractors to perform work hereunder, provided
Contractor shall fully pay said subcontractor and in all instances remain responsible for the proper
completion of this Contract.
5. Contractor shall furnish Owner appropriate releases or waivers of lien for all work
performed or materials provided at the time the next periodic payment shall be due.

6. All change orders shall be in writing and signed both by Owner and Contractor, and shall be incorporated in, and become a part of the contract.

7. Contractor warrants it is adequately insured for injury to its employees and others incurring loss or injury as a result of the acts of Contractor or its employees or subcontractors.

8. Contractor shall at its own expense obtain all permits necessary for the work to be performed.

9. Contractor agrees to remove all debris and leave the premises in broom clean condition.

10. In the event Owner shall fail to pay any periodic or installment payment due hereunder, Contractor may cease work without breach pending payment or resolution of any dispute.

11. All disputes hereunder shall be resolved by binding arbitration in accordance with rules of the American Arbitration Association.

12. Contractor shall not be liable for any delay due to circumstances beyond its control including strikes, casualty or general unavailability of materials.

13. Contractor warrants all work for a period of _____ months following completion.

ARTICLE 6.   OTHER TERMS

Signed this _____ day of _____, 19___.

Signed in the presence of:

_____   _____
Witness   Witness

By: _____   By: _____
    Owner Signature   Contractor Signature

(NOTE: IF YOU LIVE ANYWHERE OTHER THAN CALIFORNIA, THIS CONSTITUTES THE ENTIRE FORM. IF YOU LIVE IN CALIFORNIA, REPLACE THIS PAGE WITH THE FOLLOWING FOUR PAGES.)

6. All change orders shall be in writing and signed both by Owner and Contractor, and shall be incorporated in, and become a part of the contract.

7. Contractor warrants it is adequately insured for injury to its employees and others incurring loss or injury as a result of the acts of Contractor or its employees or subcontractors.

8. Contractor shall at its own expense obtain all permits necessary for the work to be performed.

9. Contractor agrees to remove all debris and leave the premises in broom clean condition.

10. In the event Owner shall fail to pay any periodic or installment payment due hereunder, Contractor may cease work without breach pending payment or resolution of any dispute.

11. All disputes hereunder shall be resolved by binding arbitration in accordance with rules of the American Arbitration Association.

12. Contractor shall not be liable for any delay due to circumstances beyond its control including strikes, casualty or general unavailability of materials.

13. Contractor warrants all work for a period of   months following completion.

> **FAILURE BY CONTRACTOR WITHOUT LAWFUL EXCUSE TO SUBSTANTIALLY COMMENCE WORK WITHIN TWENTY (20) DAYS FROM THE APPROXIMATE DATE SPECIFIED IN THE PROPOSAL AND CONTRACT WHEN WORK WILL BEGIN IS A VIOLATION OF THE CONTRACTOR'S LICENSE LAW.**

ARTICLE 6.   OTHER TERMS

1. The following terms and conditions apply to the payment schedule in Article 4:

a. If the payment schedule contained in the contract provides for a downpayment to be paid to Contractor by Owner before the commencement of work, such downpayment shall not exceed One Thousand Dollars ($1,000) or 10% of the contract price, excluding finance charges, whichever is the lesser.

b. In no event shall the payment schedule provide for Contractor to receive, nor shall Contractor actually receive, payment in excess of 100% of the value of the work performed on the project at any time, excluding finance charges, except that Contractor may receive an initial downpayment authorized by condition (a) above.

c. A failure by Contractor without lawful excuse to substantially commence work within twenty (20) days of the approximate date specified in this Contract when work will begin shall postpone the next succeeding payment to Contractor for that period of time equivalent to the time between when substantial commencement was to have occurred and when it did occur.

d. The terms and conditions set forth in sub-paragraphs (a), (b), and (c) above pertaining to the payment schedule shall not apply when the contract provides for Contractor to furnish a performance and payment bond, lien and completion bond, bond equivalent, or joint control approved by the Registrar of Contractors covering full performance and completion of the contract and such bonds or joint control is or are furnished by Contractor, or when the parties agree for full payment to be made upon or for a schedule of payments to commence after satisfactory completion of the project.

e. If the contract provides for a payment of a salesperson's commission out of the contract price, that payment shall be made on a pro rata basis in proportion to the schedule of payments made to the contractor by the disbursing party.

2. WARNING:

a. Do not use this form if the Owner is going to pay interest or any finance charge. A Home Improvement Contract with finance charges must comply both with the California Retail Installment Sales (Unruh) Act and the Federal Truth in Lending Act. The Federal Truth in Lending Act also applies if the contract price is payable in more than four installments, even if there are no interest or finance charges. (Note: Progress payments are not installment payments.)

b. Do not use this form if this is a contract for construction of a swimming pool.

NOTICE TO OWNER
(Section 7018.5—Contractors License Law)

THE LAW REQUIRES THAT, BEFORE A LICENSED CONTRACTOR CAN ENTER INTO A CONTRACT WITH YOU FOR A WORK OF IMPROVEMENT ON YOUR PROPERTY, HE MUST GIVE YOU A COPY OF THIS NOTICE.

Under the California Mechanics' Lien Law, any contractor, subcontractor, laborer, supplier, or other person or entity who helps to improve your property, but is not paid for his or her work or supplies, has a right to place a lien on your home, land, or property where the work was performed and to sue you in court to obtain payment.

This means that after a court hearing, your home, land, and property could be sold by a court officer and the proceeds of the sale used to satisfy what you owe. This can happen even if you have paid your contractor in full if the contractor's subcontractors, laborers, or suppliers remain unpaid.

To preserve their rights to file a claim or lien against your property, certain claimants such as subcontractors or material suppliers are each required to provide you with a document called a "Preliminary Notice." Contractors and laborers who contract with owners directly do not have to provide such notice since you are aware of their existence as an owner. A preliminary notice is not a lien against your property. Its purpose is to notify you of persons or entities that may have a right to file a lien against your property if they are not paid. In order to perfect their lien rights, a contractor, subcontractor, supplier, or laborer must file a mechanics' lien with the county recorder which then becomes a recorded lien against your property. Generally, the maximum time allowed for filing a mechanics' lien against your property is 90 days after substantial completion of your project.

TO INSURE EXTRA PROTECTION FOR YOURSELF AND YOUR PROPERTY, YOU MAY WISH TO TAKE ONE OR MORE OF THE FOLLOWING STEPS:

(1) Require that your contractor supply you with a payment and performance bond (not a license bond), which provides that the bonding company will either complete the project or pay damages up to the amount of the bond. This payment and performance bond as well as a copy of the construction contract should be filed with the county recorder for your further protection. The payment and performance bond will usually cost from 1 to 5 percent of the contract amount depending on the contractor's bonding ability. If a contractor cannot obtain such bonding, it may indicate his or her financial incapacity.

(2) Require that payments be made directly to subcontractors and material suppliers through a joint control. Funding services may be available, for a fee, in your area which will establish voucher or other means of payment to your contractor. These services may also provide you with lien waivers and other forms of protection. Any joint control agreement should include the addendum approved by the registrar.

CALIFORNIA ONLY

(3) Issue joint checks for payment, made out to both your Contractor and subcontractors or material suppliers involved in the project. The joint checks should be made payable to the persons or entities which send preliminary notices to you. Those persons or entities have indicated that they may have lien rights on your property, therefore you need to protect yourself. This will help to insure that all persons due payment are actually paid.

(4) Upon making payment on any completed phase of the project, and before making any further payments, require your contractor to provide you with unconditional "Waiver and Release" forms signed by each material supplier, subcontractor, and laborer involved in that portion of the work for which payment was made. The statutory lien releases are set forth in exact language in Section 3262 of the Civil Code. Most stationery stores will sell the "Waiver and Release" forms if your contractor does not have them. The material suppliers, subcontractors, and laborers that you obtain releases from are those persons or entities who have filed preliminary notices with you. If you are not certain of the material suppliers, subcontractors, and laborers working on your project, you may obtain a list from your contractor. On projects involving improvements to a single-family residence or a duplex owned by individuals, the persons signing these releases lose the right to file a mechanics' lien claim against your property. In other types of construction, this protection may still be important, but may not be as complete.

(a) To protect yourself under this option, you must be certain that all material suppliers, subcontractors, and laborers have signed the "Waiver and Release" form. If a mechanics' lien has been filed against your property, it can only be voluntarily released by a recorded "Release of Mechanics' Lien" signed by the person or entity that filed the mechanics' lien against your property unless the lawsuit to enforce the lien was not timely filed. You should not make any final payments until any and all such liens are removed. You should consult an attorney if a lien is filed against your property."

(b) Each contractor licensed under this chapter, prior to entering into a contract with an owner for work specified as home improvement pursuant to Section 7159, shall give a copy of this "Notice to Owner" to the owner, the owner's agent, or the payer. The failure to provide this notice as required shall constitute grounds for disciplinary action.

Contractors are required by law to be licensed by the Contractors' State License Board. Any questions concerning a contractor may be referred to the Registrar of the Board, Contractors' State License Board, P.O. Box 26000, Sacramento, CA 95826.

NOTICE TO OWNER OR TENANT: You have the right to require Contractor to have a performance and payment bond.

Name and Registration No. of any Salesperson who solicited or negotiated this contract:

Signed this   day of   , 19   .

Signed in the presence of:

_____   _____
Witness   Witness

_____   _____
Name of Owner   Name of Contractor

By: _____   By: _____
Owner Signature   Contractor Signature

                                         _____
                                         Street Address

                                         _____
                                         City/State/Zip

                                         _____
                                         Telephone No.

                                         _____
                                         Contractor's State License No.

CALIFORNIA ONLY

CORPORATE ACKNOWLEDGEMENT

STATE OF   }
COUNTY OF

On the   day of   , 19   , before me personally appeared

          , who being by me duly sworn, did depose and say that he is

the   of   , the corporation described in and

which executed the annexed document; that he knows the seal of said corporation; that the seal

affixed is such corporate seal; that it was so affixed by order of the Board of Directors of said

corporation, and that he signed his name thereto by like order.

On   before me,   , personally appeared
          , personally known to me (or
proved to me on the basis of satisfactory evidence) to be the person(s) whose name(s) is/are
subscribed to the within instrument and acknowledged to me that he/she/they executed the same in
his/her/their authorized capacity(ies), and that by his/her/their signature(s) on the instrument the
person(s), or the entity upon behalf of which the person(s) acted, executed the instrument.
WITNESS my hand and official seal.

Signature_____

                         Affiant   _____Known   _____Unknown
                         ID Produced_____
                                               (Seal)

COVENANT NOT TO SUE

For good and valuable consideration received, the undersigned being the holder of an actual, asserted or prospective claim against _____ arising from:

do hereby covenant that I/we shall not commence or maintain any suit thereon against said party whether at law or in equity provided nothing in this agreement constitutes a release of this or any other party thereto.

This covenant shall be binding upon and inure to the benefit of the parties, their successors, assigns and executors, administrators, personal representatives and heirs.

The undersigned affixes and seals this _____ day of _____, 19____.

Signed in the presence of:

_____   _____

Witness

STATE OF   }
COUNTY OF   }

On _____ before me, _____, personally appeared
_____, personally known to me (or proved to me on the basis of satisfactory evidence) to be the person(s) whose name(s) is/are subscribed to the within instrument and acknowledged to me that he/she/they executed the same in his/her/their authorized capacity(ies), and that by his/her/their signature(s) on the instrument the person(s), or the entity upon behalf of which the person(s) acted, executed the instrument. WITNESS my hand and official seal.

Signature_____

Affiant _____Known _____Unknown
ID Produced_____
(Seal)

CREDIT INFORMATION REQUEST

Date:

To:

Dear

Thank you for your recent order dated _____ , 19 .

We shall be pleased to consider you for a line of credit, however, we first require additional information.

Accordingly, would you please provide us with the information checked?

_____ Bank Affiliations

_____ Credit Application (enclosed)

_____ Current Financial Statements

_____ (   ) Trade References and Bank References

_____ Dun and Bradstreet or Other Credit Reporting Rating

_____ Other:_____

Pending receipt of this information we suggest C.O.D. or advance payment of $ _____ on this order to expedite prompt shipment. Upon receipt we shall immediately ship your order.

A self-addressed return envelope is enclosed for your convenience. Of course, all credit information submitted shall be held in strict confidence.

Very truly,

_____

CREDIT INTERCHANGE

Date:

To:

Re:

Dear

    This letter is in reply to your request for credit information on the above captioned account. Accordingly, we submit the following information:

1.   We have sold the account since_____

2.   The account's present balance is:

Under 30 days	$_____
30-60 days	$_____
60-90 days	$_____
Over 90 days	$_____
Total Owed	$_____

3.   We currently ship the account on the following credit terms:

4.   Other credit information:

    We are pleased we could be of service to you and trust this information shall be held in strict confidence.

Very truly,

_____

CREDITOR'S AFFIDAVIT

I, _____ of _____, the undersigned, being of age, do of my own personal knowledge make the following statements and declare them to be true.

1.   That I am _____ of _____, Plaintiff in this action, and have custody of its book and records.

2.   That according to said books and records, and my own personal knowledge, Defendant is justly indebted to Plaintiff in the amount of $_____ without setoff or defense.

3.   That despite repeated demand for payment, no payment has been received.

4.   That there is no insurance coverage or other posted security from which to satisfy this claim.

Signed under the pains and penalties of perjury this _____ day of _____, 19____ .

STATE OF _____   }
COUNTY OF _____

On _____ before me, _____, personally appeared _____, personally known to me (or proved to me on the basis of satisfactory evidence) to be the person(s) whose name(s) is/are subscribed to the within instrument and acknowledged to me that he/she/they executed the same in his/her/their authorized capacity(ies), and that by his/her/their signature(s) on the instrument the person(s), or the entity upon behalf of which the person(s) acted, executed the instrument. WITNESS my hand and official seal.

Signature_____

Affiant   _____Known   _____Unknown
ID Produced_____
(Seal)

DAMAGED GOODS ACCEPTANCE

Date:

To:

Dear

    We have received defective or non-conforming goods on our order dated   ,
19 . The defective items are as follows:

    We shall accept said goods provided we are allowed a price deduction of $.

    Please advise immediately, as we shall otherwise be required to return said goods at your expense, reserving such rights and remedies as we have under the Uniform Commercial Code.

Very truly,

_____

DEBT ACKNOWLEDGEMENT

The undersigned hereby confirms and acknowledges to

(Creditor) that the undersigned is indebted to the Creditor in the amount of $

as of date hereof, which amount is due and owing and includes all accrued interest and other

permitted charges to date. We further acknowledge that there are no defenses to, or credits or

rights of set off as against said account balance and that the Creditor shall be authorized to enter

a confession of judgment (where so allowed by law) against the undersigned for the amount of

debt acknowledged to be due.

Signed this   day of   , 19   .

Signed in the presence of:

_____   _____
Witness   Debtor

DEBT RE-AFFIRMATION

FOR GOOD AND VALUABLE CONSIDERATION RECEIVED, the undersigned hereby acknowledges and re-affirms to

(Creditor) and its successors and assigns, a certain prior debt discharged, released, extinguished or cancelled pursuant to   and that the undersigned shall be and agrees to remain bound on said debt in the amount of $ only and for no greater sum, and to the same extent as if said debt to the amount stated were not discharged in the first instance.

It is further agreed that the above stated re-affirmed debt shall be paid in the following manner:

In addition, if said debt was discharged pursuant to any provision of the United States Bankruptcy Code, the Undersigned shall diligently make application (before the United States Bankruptcy Court) for said approval.

This agreement shall be binding upon the parties, their successors, assigns and personal representatives.

Signed this   day of   , 19   .

In the presence of:

_____   _____
Witness   Debtor

DECLARATION OF TRUST

This declaration of trust is made on   , 19   , by

          ("Trustee") in favor of

("Beneficiary").

          The Trustee solemnly declares that he or she holds

                              ("Property") in trust

solely for the benefit of said Beneficiary.

          The Trustee further promises the Beneficiary:

      (a)   not to deal with the Property in any way, except to transfer it to the Beneficiary, without the authorization of the Beneficiary; and,

      (b)   to account to the Beneficiary for any money received by the Trustee, other than from Beneficiary, in connection with holding said Property.

Signed in the presence of:

_____   _____

Witness   Trustee

DEFECTIVE GOODS NOTICE

Date:

To:

Dear

Please be advised we are in receipt of goods shipped to us under your Invoice or Order No.   , dated   , 19   .

Certain goods as listed on the attached sheet are defective or non-conforming to our order for the following reasons:

Accordingly, we reject said goods and demand credit or adjustment in the amount of $, representing the billed amount for said items. We also intend to re-ship said goods to you at your expense.

Please confirm the credit and also issue instructions for the return of said goods.

You are advised by this notice that we reserve such further rights as we may have under the Uniform Commercial Code or applicable law.

We anticipate your prompt reply.

Very truly,

_____

DEMAND FOR CONTRIBUTION

Date:

To:

On   , 19   , the undersigned made payment in the amount of

dollars ($) to

for   .

Said payment is covered by our agreement dated   , 19   , requiring

contribution in the event of

.

Accordingly, the undersigned makes demand upon you for contribution in the amount of

dollars ($).

_____

DEMAND FOR DELIVERY

Date:

To:

Dear

    The undersigned has made full payment to you in the sum of $ for certain goods to be shipped by you pursuant to our accepted order dated   , 19 . We demand delivery of said goods in accordance with our order, since said goods have not been received as per terms of our order.

    Unless said goods are received by us on or before   , 19 , we shall consider you to be in breach of contract and we shall thereupon expect a full refund, reserving such further rights as we have under the Uniform Commercial Code, for any other damages sustained.

    We shall appreciate immediate notification of your intentions on this matter.

Very truly,

_____

DEMAND FOR INSPECTION OF
CORPORATE BOOKS AND RECORDS

The undersigned, _____ , is the holder of

shares of the common stock of

and does hereby demand the opportunity to inspect, at the office of the Corporation, the books

and records of the Corporation, its stock ledger and the list of its shareholders. The undersigned

does further state that the inspection is sought for a proper purpose, to wit:

The undersigned also states that he has never sold nor offered for sale any list of

shareholders of any corporation, nor assisted any person in obtaining such a list or record for

such purposes.

The requested date and time for inspection is:

Date: _____

Time: _____

_____
Shareholder

STATE OF
COUNTY OF   }

On _____ before me, _____ , personally appeared
_____ , personally known to me (or
proved to me on the basis of satisfactory evidence) to be the person(s) whose name(s) is/are
subscribed to the within instrument and acknowledged to me that he/she/they executed the same
in his/her/their authorized capacity(ies), and that by his/her/their signature(s) on the instrument
the person(s), or the entity upon behalf of which the person(s) acted, executed the instrument.
WITNESS my hand and official seal.

Signature_____

Affiant _____Known _____Unknown
ID Produced_____
(Seal)

DEMAND FOR PAYMENT

Date:

To:

Dear

    We have tried several times to resolve the problem of your past due account, but the problem continues. Your account remains seriously overdue in the amount of $.

    This is your final notice. Unless we have your check for

dollars $ within ten (10) days, we shall immediately turn your account over to our attorneys for collection.

    We believe you'll agree that immediate payment is in your own best interest as it will save you added interest and court costs, and help preserve your credit rating.

Very truly,

_____

DEMAND FOR RENT

Date:

To:

     Demand is hereby made that you pay to the undersigned

dollars ($), which represents past rent as of   . This sum shall

be paid on or before   , or the lease agreement between us shall be

declared forfeited and I shall demand surrender of the demised premises by you as provided in

Section   of a certain lease agreement between us dated   .

                    _____

DEMAND NOTE

$ Date:

On demand, the undersigned, for value received, jointly and severally promises to pay to the order of   the sum of

dollars ($) together with interest thereon from the date hereof until paid at the rate of   % per annum.

In the event this note is not paid when due, the undersigned shall pay all attorney's fees and reasonable costs of collection.

_____

Witnessed:

_____

DEMAND ON GUARANTOR FOR PAYMENT

Date:

To:

Dear

  The undersigned is the holder of your guaranty dated   , 19   ,
wherein you guaranteed the debt owed us by

                     .

  Please be advised that said debt is in default. Accordingly, demand is made upon you as a
guarantor for full payment on the outstanding debt due us in the amount of $.

  In the event payment is not made within   (   ) days, we shall proceed
to enforce our rights against you under the guaranty. We shall additionally hold you responsible
for attorneys fees, costs of collection and further interest as may accrue.

               Very truly,

_____
Name

_____
Address

_____

DEMAND PROMISSORY NOTE

$ Date:

      FOR VALUE RECEIVED, the undersigned jointly and severally promise to pay to the order of   , the sum of

Dollars ($), together with interest of   % per annum on the unpaid balance. The entire unpaid principal and any accrued interest shall be fully and immediately payable UPON DEMAND of any holder thereof.

      Upon default in making payment within   days of demand, and provided this note is turned over for collection, the undersigned agree to pay all reasonable legal fees and costs of collection to the extent permitted by law. This note shall take effect as a sealed instrument and be enforced in accordance with the laws of the payee's state. All parties to this note waive presentment, notice of non-payment, protest and notice of protest, and agree to remain fully bound notwithstanding the release of any party, extension or modification of terms, or discharge of any collateral for this note.

In the presence of:

_____   _____
Witness   Debtor

                                              _____
                                              Debtor

DEMAND TO ACKNOWLEDGE SHIPPING DATES

Date:

To:

Dear

     We request that you confirm and specify shipping arrangements pursuant to our order of

          , 19   , and that you furnish us timely assurance that you shall

comply with its terms.

     Failure to provide sufficient assurance shall constitute a breach of said contract and we

shall no longer consider ourselves obligated under said contract. Further, we shall hold you

responsible for all resultant damages as provided under the Uniform Commercial Code.

     Please acknowledge confirmed shipping dates, in writing, no later than   ,

19 .

                 Very truly,

_____

DEMAND TO ENDORSER FOR PAYMENT

Date:

To:

Please be advised that the undersigned is the holder of the below described instrument on which you are an endorser.

Maker:

Date:

Face Amount:

Notice is hereby provided that said instrument has been dishonored and has not been paid, and protest and demand is hereby made upon you to immediately pay the amount due in the amount of $.

In the event payment is not made within five days, the undersigned shall commence suit on your warranties of endorsement.

Upon full payment on your endorsement, we shall assign to you all our rights, title and interest as we have to the instrument.

Very truly,

_____

CERTIFIED MAIL, Return Receipt Requested

DEMAND TO PAY PROMISSORY NOTE

Date:

To:

Dear

Reference is made to a certain promissory note dated , 19 , in the original principal amount of $ and to which the undersigned is holder.

You are in default under said note in that the following payment(s) have not been made.

Payment Date	Amount Due

Accordingly, demand is hereby made for full payment of the entire balance of $ due under the note. In the event payment is not received within days, this note shall be forwarded to our attorneys for collection and you shall additionally be liable for all reasonable cost of collection.

Very truly,

_____

DIRECT DEPOSIT AUTHORIZATION

Name:_____

I.D.#_____

S.S.#_____

Bank Name & Branch:_____

Account Number:_____

Check appropriate box:

_____ Direct deposit.

The undersigned hereby requests and authorizes the entire amount of my paycheck each pay period to be deposited directly into the bank account named above.

_____ Direct payroll deduction deposit.

The undersigned hereby requests and authorizes the sum of _____ _____ dollars ($_____) be deducted from my paycheck each pay period and to be deposited directly into the bank account named above.

_____ I would like to cancel my deposit authorization:

The undersigned hereby cancels the authorization for direct deposit or payroll deduction deposit previously submitted.

Employee Signature_____Date_____

Please attach a copy of deposit slip.

DISCHARGE OF MORTGAGE

BE IT KNOWN, that for value received, we   ,

of   holders of a certain real

estate mortgage from   to   ,

said mortgage dated   , 19   , and recorded in Book or Volume   , Page

           , of the   County Registry of Deeds, acknowledge full satisfaction

and discharge of same.

Signed under seal this   day of   , 19   .

_____

_____

STATE OF   }
COUNTY OF

On   before me,   , personally appeared
                                    , personally known to me (or
proved to me on the basis of satisfactory evidence) to be the person(s) whose name(s) is/are
subscribed to the within instrument and acknowledged to me that he/she/they executed the same
in his/her/their authorized capacity(ies), and that by his/her/their signature(s) on the instrument
the person(s), or the entity upon behalf of which the person(s) acted, executed the instrument.
WITNESS my hand and official seal.

Signature_____

Affiant _____Known _____Unknown
ID Produced_____
(Seal)

DISCIPLINARY NOTICE

Employee_____

Department_____

_____ Written Warning   _____ Final Warning

1. Statement of the problem:_____

_____

_____

2. Prior discussion or warnings on this subject, whether oral or written:

_____

_____

3. Company policy on this subject:_____

_____

_____

4. Summary of corrective action to be taken by the Company and/or employee:

_____

_____

5. Consequences of failure to improve performance or correct behavior:

_____

_____

6. Employee statement:_____

_____

_____

Employee Signature:_____ Date_____

Management Approval:_____ Date_____

Distribution: One copy to Employee, one copy to Supervisor and original to Personnel File.

DISHONORED CHECK PLACED FOR BANK COLLECTION

Date:

To:

Dear

      We hereby enclose and place with you for collection and credit to our account the below described check previously returned to us due to insufficient/uncollected funds:

          Maker:

          Date of Check:

          Check Number:

          Amount:

          Drawee Bank:

      Please charge our account your customary service fee for handling this check on a collection basis.

      We would appreciate notification when the check clears, or prompt return of said check to us should the check remain unpaid beyond the collection period.

      Thank you for your cooperation.

                     Very truly,

_____

DISPUTED ACCOUNT SETTLEMENT

Settlement Agreement by and between

of   (Creditor) and

of   (Debtor).

Whereas, Creditor asserts to hold a certain claim against Debtor in the amount of

$ arising from the below described transaction:

And whereas, Debtor disputes said claim, and denies said debt is due.

And whereas, the parties desire to resolve and forever settle and adjust said claim.

Now, therefore, Debtor agrees to pay to Creditor and Creditor agrees to accept from Debtor simultaneous herewith, the sum of

$ in full payment, settlement, satisfaction, discharge and release of said claim and in release of any further claims thereto. Creditor acknowledges that there shall be no adverse report filed against Debtor with any credit bureau.

This agreement shall be binding upon and inure to the benefit of the parties, their successors, assigns and personal representatives.

Signed this   day of   , 19   .

Witnesseth:

_____   _____
Witness   Creditor

_____   _____
Witness   Debtor

DISSOLUTION OF CORPORATION

CERTIFICATE

_____

      We, the President, and Secretary of   , in accordance with

the requirements of the Corporation Laws of the State of   and in order to obtain

the dissolution of said Corporation, as provided by said Law,

DO HEREBY CERTIFY AS FOLLOWS:

      The registered office of   (Corporation) in the State of

      is at   , and the resident

agent thereof, upon whom process against this Corporation may be served, is

at

      The dissolution of said Corporation has been duly authorized in accordance with the

provisions of the Corporation Laws of the State of   .

      The following is a list of the names and residences of the directors of the said

Corporation:

Name	Address
_____	_____
	_____
_____	_____
	_____
_____	_____
	_____

The following is a list of the names and residence addresses of the officers of the Corporation:

Name	Office	Residence
_____	_____	_____
		_____
_____	_____	_____
		_____
_____	_____	_____
		_____
_____	_____	_____
		_____

A True Record

Attest

_____
President

_____
Secretary

DURABLE POWER OF ATTORNEY

NOTICE: THIS IS AN IMPORTANT DOCUMENT. BEFORE SIGNING THIS DOCUMENT, YOU SHOULD KNOW THESE IMPORTANT FACTS. THE PURPOSE OF THIS POWER OF ATTORNEY IS TO GIVE THE PERSON WHOM YOU DESIGNATE (YOUR "AGENT") BROAD POWERS TO HANDLE YOUR PROPERTY, WHICH MAY INCLUDE POWERS TO PLEDGE, SELL OR OTHERWISE DISPOSE OF ANY REAL OR PERSONAL PROPERTY WITHOUT ADVANCE NOTICE TO YOU OR APPROVAL BY YOU. YOU MAY SPECIFY THAT THESE POWERS WILL EXIST EVEN AFTER YOU BECOME DISABLED, INCAPACITATED OR INCOMPETENT. THIS DOCUMENT DOES NOT AUTHORIZE ANYONE TO MAKE MEDICAL OR OTHER HEALTH CARE DECISIONS FOR YOU. IF THERE IS ANYTHING ABOUT THIS FORM THAT YOU DO NOT UNDERSTAND, YOU SHOULD ASK A LAWYER TO EXPLAIN IT TO YOU. YOU MAY REVOKE THIS POWER OF ATTORNEY IF YOU LATER WISH TO DO SO.

TO ALL PERSONS, be it known that I,   ,
of   ,
the undersigned Grantor, do hereby make and grant a general power of attorney to
                                        , of

                                                                                ,
and do thereupon constitute and appoint said individual as my attorney-in-fact.

My attorney-in-fact shall act in my name, place and stead in any way which I myself could do, if I were personally present, with respect to the following matters, to the extent that I am permitted by law to act through an agent:

(**NOTICE**: The Grantor must write his or her initials in the corresponding blank space of a box below with respect to each of the subdivisions (A) through (N) below for which the Grantor wants to give the agent authority. If the blank space within a box for any particular subdivision is NOT initialed, NO AUTHORITY WILL BE GRANTED for matters that are included in that subdivision. Cross out power withheld.

[   ]   (A) Real estate transactions
[   ]   (B) Tangible personal property transactions
[   ]   (C) Bond, share and commodity transactions
[   ]   (D) Banking transactions
[   ]   (E) Business operating transactions
[   ]   (F) Insurance transactions
[   ]   (G) Gifts to charities and individuals other than attorney-in-fact (**If trust distributions are involved or tax consequences are anticipated, consult an attorney.**)
[   ]   (H) Claims and litigation
[   ]   (I) Personal relationships and affairs
[   ]   (J) Benefits from military service
[   ]   (K) Records, reports and statements
[   ]   (L) Full and unqualified authority to my attorney-in-fact to delegate any or all of the foregoing powers to any person or persons whom my attorney-in-fact shall select
[   ]   (M) All other matters
[   ]   (N) Durable provision: If the blank space in the block to the left is initialed by the grantor, this power of attorney shall not be affected by the subsequent disability or incompetence of the Grantor.

Other Terms:

My attorney-in-fact hereby accepts this appointment subject to its terms and agrees to act and perform in said fiduciary capacity consistent with my best interests as he/she in his/her best discretion deems advisable, and I affirm and ratify all acts so undertaken.

TO INDUCE ANY THIRD PARTY TO ACT HEREUNDER, I HEREBY AGREE THAT ANY THIRD PARTY RECEIVING A DULY EXECUTED COPY OR FACSIMILE OF THIS INSTRUMENT MAY ACT HEREUNDER, AND THAT REVOCATION OR TERMINATION HEREOF SHALL BE INEFFECTIVE AS TO SUCH THIRD PARTY UNLESS AND UNTIL ACTUAL NOTICE OR KNOWLEDGE OF SUCH REVOCATION OR TERMINATION SHALL HAVE BEEN RECEIVED BY SUCH THIRD PARTY, AND I FOR MYSELF AND FOR MY HEIRS, EXECUTORS, LEGAL REPRESENTATIVES AND ASSIGNS, HEREBY AGREE TO INDEMNIFY AND HOLD HARMLESS ANY SUCH THIRD PARTY FROM AND AGAINST ANY AND ALL CLAIMS THAT MAY ARISE AGAINST SUCH THIRD PARTY BY REASON OF SUCH THIRD PARTY HAVING RELIED ON THE PROVISIONS OF THIS INSTRUMENT.

Signed under seal this   day of
                                    , 19   .

Signed in the presence of:

_____   _____
Witness   Grantor

_____   _____
Witness   Attorney-in-Fact

State of
County of   }
On   before me,   ,
appeared   ,
personally known to me (or proved to me on the basis of satisfactory evidence) to be the person(s) whose name(s) is/are subscribed to the within instrument and acknowledged to me that he/she/they executed the same in his/her/their authorized capacity(ies), and that by his/her/their signature(s) on the instrument the person(s), or the entity upon behalf of which the person(s) acted, executed the instrument.
WITNESS my hand and official seal.

Signature_____

                          Affiant _____Known_____Produced ID
                          Type of ID _____
                                                      (Seal)

EMPLOYEE AGREEMENT ON INVENTIONS AND PATENTS

Agreement made between   , hereinafter referred to as "Company," and   , hereinafter referred to as "Employee."

In consideration of the employment of Employee by Company, the parties agree as follows:

1.   Employee shall or may have possession of or access to facilities, apparatus, equipment, drawings, systems, formulae, reports, manuals, invention records, customer lists, computer programs, or other material embodying trade secrets or confidential technical or business information of Company or its Affiliates. Employee therein agrees not to use any such information or material for himself or others, and not to take any such material or reproductions thereof from Company, at any time during or after employment by Company, except as required in Employee's duties to Company. Employee agrees immediately to return all such material and reproductions thereof in his possession to Company upon request and in any event upon termination of employment.

2.   Except with prior written authorization by Company, Employee agrees not to disclose or publish any trade secret or confidential technical or business information or material of Company or its Affiliates or of another party to whom Company owes an obligation of confidence, at any time during or after employment by Company.

3.   Employee shall promptly furnish to Company a complete record of any and all inventions, patents and improvements, whether patentable or not, which he, solely or jointly, may conceive, make, or first disclose during the period of his employment by Company.

4.   Employee agrees to and does hereby grant and assign to Company or its nominee employee's entire right, title, and interest in and to inventions, patents and improvements that relate in any way to the actual or anticipated business or activities of Company or its Affiliates, or that are anticipated by or result from any task or work for or on behalf of Company together with any and all domestic and foreign patent rights in such inventions and improvements. To aid Company or its nominee in securing full benefit and protection thereof, Employee agrees promptly to do all lawful acts reasonably requested, at any time during and after employment by Company, without additional compensation but at Company's expense.

5.   Employee agrees that, in the event employee accepts employment with any firm or engages in any type of activity in employee's own behalf or in behalf of any organization following termination of his employment with Company, employee shall notify Company in writing within thirty days of the name and address of such organization and the nature of such activity.

6.   Employee agrees to give Company timely written notice of any prior employment agreements or patent rights that might conflict with the interests of Company or its Affiliates.

7.	No waiver by either party of any breach by the other party of any provision of this Agreement shall be deemed or construed to be a waiver of any succeeding breach of such provision or as a waiver of the provision itself.

8.	This Agreement shall be binding upon and pass to the benefit of the successors and assigns of Company and, insofar as the same may be applied thereto, the heirs, legal representatives, and assigns of Employee.

9.	This Agreement shall supersede the terms of any prior employment agreement or understanding between Employee and Company. This Agreement may be modified or amended only in writing signed by an executive officer of Company and by Employee.

10.	Should any portion of this Agreement be held to be invalid, unenforceable or void, such holding shall not have the effect of invalidating the remainder of this Agreement or any other part thereof, the parties hereby agreeing that the portion so held to be invalid, unenforceable, or void shall, if possible, be deemed amended or reduced in scope.

11.	This agreement shall be binding upon and inure to the benefit of the parties, their successors, assigns and personal representatives.

_____

Company Name

_____

Employee's Full Name

Employee acknowledges reading,
understanding and receiving a
signed copy of this Agreement.

By:_____

Company Officer or Witness

_____

Employee's Full Signature

EMPLOYEE COVENANT: EXPENSE RECOVERY

The undersigned, _____, (Employee) of

_____, (Employer) hereby promises the

Employer:

To reimburse the Employer all amounts paid by the Employer to the Employee as compensation for or reimbursement of expenses incurred in the course of employment that are disallowed, in whole or in part, as deductible to the Employer for income tax purposes.

Date:

Signed in the presence of:

_____   _____
Witness   Employee

EMPLOYEE NON-COMPETE AGREEMENT

For good consideration and as an inducement for
(Company) to employ   (Employee), the undersigned Employee
hereby agrees not to directly or indirectly compete with the business of the Company and its
successors and assigns during the period of employment and for a period of   years
following termination of employment and notwithstanding the cause or reason for termination.

The term "not compete" as used herein shall mean that the Employee shall not own,
manage, operate, consult to or be employed in a business substantially similar to or competitive
with the present business of the Company or such other business activity in which the Company
may substantially engage during the term of employment.

The Employee acknowledges that the Company shall or may in reliance of this
agreement provide Employee access to trade secrets, customers and other confidential data and
that the provisions of this agreement are reasonably necessary to protect the Company and its
good will. Employee agrees to retain said information as confidential and not to use said
information on his or her own behalf or disclose same to any third party.

This agreement shall be binding upon and inure to the benefit of the parties, their
successors, assigns and personal representatives.

Signed this   day of   , 19   .

_____
Company

_____
Employee

EMPLOYEE NON-DISCLOSURE AGREEMENT

FOR GOOD CONSIDERATION, and in consideration of being employed by _____ (Company), the undersigned employee hereby agrees and acknowledges:

1.   That during the course of my employ there may be disclosed to me certain trade secrets of the Company; said trade secrets consisting but not necessarily limited to:

   a)   Technical information: Methods, processes, formulae, compositions, systems, techniques, inventions, machines, computer programs and research projects.

   b)   Business information: Customer lists, pricing data, sources of supply, financial data and marketing, production, or merchandising systems or plans.

2.   I agree that I shall not during, or at any time after the termination of my employment with the Company, use for myself or others, or disclose or divulge to others including future employers, any trade secrets, confidential information, or any other proprietary data of the Company in violation of this agreement.

3.   That upon the termination of my employment from the Company:

   a)   I shall return to the Company all documents and property of the Company, including but not necessarily limited to: drawings, blueprints, reports, manuals, correspondence, customer lists, computer programs, and all other materials and all copies thereof relating in any way to the Company's business, or in any way obtained by me during the course of employ. I further agree that I shall not retain any copies, notes or abstracts of the foregoing.

   b)   The Company may notify any future or prospective employer or third party of the existence of this agreement, and shall be entitled to full injunctive relief for any breach.

c)   This agreement shall be binding upon me and my personal representatives and successors in interest, and shall inure to the benefit of the Company, its successors and assigns.

Signed this   day of   , 19   .

_____

Company

_____

Employee

EMPLOYEE WARNING

Date:

To: (Employee)

You are hereby advised that your work performance is unsatisfactory for the following reasons:

We expect immediate correction of the problem otherwise we shall have no alternative but to consider termination of your employment.

If there is any question about this notice or if we can help you improve your performance or correct the difficulties, then please discuss this matter with your supervisor, at the earliest possible opportunity.

_____

EMPLOYMENT AGREEMENT

Employment Agreement, between   (the "Company") and   (the "Employee").

1.   For good consideration, the Company employees the Employee on the following terms and conditions.

2.   Term of Employment. Subject to the provisions for termination set forth below this agreement will begin on   , 19   , unless sooner terminated.

3.   Salary. The Company shall pay Employee a salary of $ per year, for the services of the Employee, payable at regular payroll periods.

4.   Duties and Position. The Company hires the Employee in the capacity of   . The Employee's duties may be reasonably modified at the Company's discretion from time to time.

5.   Employee to Devote Full Time to Company. The Employee will devote full time, attention, and energies to the business of the Company, and, during this employment, will not engage in any other business activity, regardless of whether such activity is pursued for profit, gain, or other pecuniary advantage. Employee is not prohibited from making personal investments in any other businesses provided those investments do not require active involvement in the operation of said companies.

6.   Confidentiality of Proprietary Information. Employee agrees, during or after the term of this employment, not to reveal confidential information, or trade secrets to any person, firm, corporation, or entity. Should Employee reveal or threaten to reveal this information, the Company shall be entitled to an injunction restraining the Employee from disclosing same, or from rendering any services to any entity to whom said information has been or is threatened to be disclosed. The right to secure an injunction is not exclusive, and the Company may pursue any other remedies it has against the Employee for a breach or threatened breach of this condition, including the recovery of damages from the Employee.

7.   Reimbursement of Expenses. The Employee may incur reasonable expenses for furthering the Company's business, including expenses for entertainment, travel, and similar items. The Company shall reimburse Employee for all business expenses after the Employee presents an itemized account of expenditures, pursuant to Company policy.

8.   Vacation. The Employee shall be entitled to a yearly vacation of   weeks at full pay.

9.   Disability. If Employee cannot perform the duties because of illness or incapacity for a period of more than   weeks, the compensation otherwise due during said illness or incapacity will be reduced by   (   ) percent. The Employee's full

compensation will be reinstated upon return to work. However, if the Employee is absent from work for any reason for a continuous period of over _____ months, the Company may terminate the Employee's employment, and the Company's obligations under this agreement will cease on that date.

10.   Termination of Agreement. Without cause, the Company may terminate this agreement at any time upon _____ days' written notice to the Employee. If the Company requests, the Employee will continue to perform his/her duties and be paid his/her regular salary up to the date of termination. In addition, the Company will pay the Employee on the date of termination a severance allowance of $ _____ less taxes and social security required to be withheld. Without cause, the Employee may terminate employment upon _____ days' written notice to the Company. Employee may be required to perform his or her duties and will be paid the regular salary to date of termination but shall not receive a severance allowance. Notwithstanding anything to the contrary contained in this agreement, the Company may terminate the Employee's employment upon _____ days' notice to the Employee should any of the following events occur:

a)   The sale of substantially all of the Company's assets to a single purchaser or group of associated purchasers; or

b)   The sale, exchange, or other disposition, in one transaction of the majority of the Company's outstanding corporate shares; or

c)   The Company's decision to terminate its business and liquidate its assets;

d)   The merger or consolidation of the Company with another company.

e)   Bankruptcy or chapter 11 reorganization.

11.   Death Benefit. Should Employee die during the term of employment, the Company shall pay to Employee's estate any compensation due through the end of the month in which death occurred.

12.   Restriction on Post Employment Competition. For a period of _____
(   ) years after the end of employment, the Employee shall not control, consult to or be employed by any business similar to that conducted by the Company, either by soliciting any of its accounts or by operating within Employer's general trading area.

13.   Assistance in Litigation. Employee shall upon reasonable notice, furnish such information and proper assistance to the Company as it may reasonably require in connection with any litigation in which it is, or may become, a party either during or after employment.

14.   Effect of Prior Agreements. This agreement supersedes any prior agreement between the Company or any predecessor of the Company and the Employee, except that this agreement shall not affect or operate to reduce any benefit or compensation inuring to the Employee of a kind elsewhere provided and not expressly provided in this agreement.

15.   Settlement by Arbitration. Any claim or controversy that arises out of or relates to this agreement, or the breach of it, shall be settled by arbitration in accordance with the rules of the American Arbitration Association. Judgment upon the award rendered may be entered in any court with jurisdiction.

16.   Limited Effect of Waiver by Company. Should Company waive breach of any provision of this agreement by the Employee, that waiver will not operate or be construed as a waiver of further breach by the Employee.

17.   Severability. If, for any reason, any provision of this agreement is held invalid, all other provisions of this agreement shall remain in effect. If this agreement is held invalid or cannot be enforced, then to the full extent permitted by law any prior agreement between the Company (or any predecessor thereof) and the Employee shall be deemed reinstated as if this agreement had not been executed.

18.   Assumption of Agreement by Company's Successors and Assignees. The Company's rights and obligations under this agreement will inure to the benefit and be binding upon the Company's successors and assignees.

19.   Oral Modifications Not Binding. This instrument is the entire agreement of the Company and the Employee. Oral changes shall have no effect. It may be altered only by a written agreement signed by the party against whom enforcement of any waiver, change, modification, extension, or discharge is sought.

Signed this   day of   , 19   .

_____   _____
Witness   Company Representative

_____   _____
Witness   Employee

ESCROW AGREEMENT

AGREEMENT between   , (Seller)
                                                                              ,(Buyer) and
                          (Escrow Agent).

Simultaneously with the making of this Agreement, Seller and Buyer have entered into a contract (the Contract) by which Seller will sell to Buyer the following property:

The closing will take place on   , 19   , at   .m., at the offices of
                                        , located at
, or at such other time and place as Seller and Buyer may jointly designate in writing. Pursuant to the Contract, Buyer must deposit $ as a down payment to be held in escrow by Escrow Agent.

The $ down payment referred to hereinabove has been paid by Buyer to Escrow Agent. Escrow Agent acknowledges receipt of $ from Buyer by check, subject to collection.

If the closing takes place under the Contract, Escrow Agent at the time of closing shall pay the amount deposited with Agent to Seller or in accordance with Seller's written instructions. Escrow Agent shall make simultaneous transfer of the said property to the Buyer.

If no closing takes place under the Contract, Escrow Agent shall continue to hold the amount deposited until receipt of written authorization for its disposition signed by both Buyer and Seller. If there is any dispute as to whom Escrow Agent is to deliver the amount deposited, Escrow Agent shall hold the sum until the parties' rights are finally determined in an appropriate action or proceeding or until a court orders Escrow Agent to deposit the down payment with it. If Escrow Agent does not receive a proper written authorization from Seller and Buyer, or if an action or proceeding to determine Seller's and Buyer's rights is not begun or diligently prosecuted, Escrow Agent is under no obligation to bring an action or proceeding in court to deposit the sum held, but may continue to hold the deposit.

Escrow Agent assumes no liability except that of a stakeholder. Escrow Agent's duties are limited to those specifically set out in this Agreement. Escrow Agent shall incur no liability to anyone except for willful misconduct or gross negligence so long as the Escrow Agent acts in good faith. Seller and Buyer release Escrow Agent from any act done or omitted in good faith in the performance of Escrow Agent's duties.

Special provisions:

Whereof the parties sign their names this   day of   , 19   .

Signed in the presence of:

_____   _____
Witness   Seller

_____   _____
Witness   Buyer

_____   _____
Witness   Escrow Agent

EXCEPTIONS TO PURCHASE ORDER

Date:

To:

Dear

    We are in receipt of your Purchase Order No.   dated   , 19 .

    We confirm acceptance of said order subject only to the following exceptions:

    On exceptions noted, we shall assume you agree to same unless objection is received within ten (10) days of your receipt of this notice. We shall promptly ship such goods as are not subject to exception.

    Thank you for your business and we trust you understand the reasons for the exceptions.

             Very truly,

_____

EXCLUSIVE RIGHT TO SELL

For and in consideration of your services to be rendered in listing for sale and in undertaking to sell or find a purchaser for the property hereinafter described, the parties understand and agree that this is an exclusive listing to sell the real estate located at:

,

together with the following improvements and fixtures:

The minimum selling price of the property shall be

dollars ($), to be payable on the following terms:

You are authorized to accept and hold a deposit in the amount of

dollars ($) as a deposit and to apply such deposit on the purchase price.

If said property is sold, traded or in any other way disposed of either by us or by anyone else within the time specified in this listing, it is agreed to and understood that you shall receive from the sale or trade of said property as your commission   percent (%) of the purchase price. Should said property be sold or traded within   days after expiration of this listing agreement to a purchaser with whom you have been negotiating for the sale or trade of the property, the said commission shall be due and payable on demand.

We agree to furnish a certificate of title showing a good and merchantable title of record, and further agree to convey by good and sufficient warranty deed or guaranteed title on payment in full.

This listing contract shall continue until midnight of   , 19   .

Date:

_____

Owner

_____

Owner

I accept this listing and agree to act promptly and diligently to procure a buyer for said property.

Date:

_____

EXERCISE OF OPTION

Date:

To:

      You are hereby notified that the undersigned has elected to and does hereby exercise and accept the option dated   , 19   , executed by you as seller to the undersigned as purchaser, and agrees to all terms, conditions, and provisions of the option.

                                         _____

EXTENSION OF AGREEMENT

Extension of Agreement made by and between   (First Party),
and   (Second Party), said agreement being dated   ,
19   (Agreement).

Whereas said Agreement expires on   , 19   , and the parties desire to
extend and continue said agreement; it is provided that said Agreement shall be extended for an
additional term commencing upon the expiration of the original term with the new term expiring
on   , 19   .

This extension shall be on the same terms and conditions as contained in the original
agreement and as if set forth and incorporated herein excepting only for the following
modification to the original agreement;

This extension of Agreement shall be binding upon and inure to the benefit of the parties,
their successors and assigns.

Signed this   day of   , 19   .

In the presence of:

_____   _____
Witness   First Party

_____   _____
Witness   Second Party

EXTENSION OF LEASE

Extension of Lease Agreement made by and between   (Landlord), and   (Tenant) relative to a certain lease agreement for premises known as   , and dated   , 19   (Lease).

For good consideration, Landlord and Tenant each agree to extend the term of said Lease for a period of   years commencing on   , 19   , and terminating on   , 19   , with no further right of renewal or extension beyond said termination date.

During the extended term, Tenant shall pay Lessor rent of $ per annum, payable $ per month in advance.

Other terms are as follows:

It is further provided, however, that all other terms of the Lease shall continue during this extended term as if set forth herein.

This agreement shall be binding upon and shall inure to the benefit of the parties, their successors, assigns and personal representatives.

Signed this   day of   , 19   .

Witnessed:

_____   _____
Witness   Landlord

_____   _____
Witness   Tenant

FICTITIOUS OR ASSUMED NAME CERTIFICATE
BY A CORPORATION

CERTIFICATE

The following is hereby certified:

1. Business is, or will be, transacted at:

, under the   name of

, a corporation incorporated under the laws of   (state), and

authorized to transact business in the State of   , with its main office located at:

2. The nature of the business is:

3. The corporation is the sole owner of the business and no other corporation or entity is interested in the conduct of said business.

This certificate is executed and filed pursuant to:

Date: _____

STATE OF   }
COUNTY OF   }

On   before me,   , personally appeared
, personally known to me (or proved to me on the basis of satisfactory evidence) to be the person(s) whose name(s) is/are subscribed to the within instrument and acknowledged to me that he/she/they executed the same in his/her/their authorized capacity(ies), and that by his/her/their signature(s) on the instrument the person(s), or the entity upon behalf of which the person(s) acted, executed the instrument. WITNESS my hand and official seal.

Signature_____

Affiant _____Known _____Unknown
ID Produced_____
(Seal)

*NOTE: If you live in New York State, call the New York State Department of Corporation for the official form.

FICTITIOUS OR ASSUMED NAME CERTIFICATE
BY AN INDIVIDUAL

CERTIFICATE

The undersigned hereby certifies the following:

1. The undersigned is, or will be carrying on business at:

2. The real name and address of the undersigned is:

3. The undersigned is of full age, and no other person is interested as a partner, part owner, or otherwise in the business or conduct of it.

4. The nature of the business is:

This certificate is executed and filed pursuant to:

Date: _____

STATE OF
COUNTY OF   }

On   before me,   , personally appeared
, personally known to me (or proved to me on the basis of satisfactory evidence) to be the person(s) whose name(s) is/are subscribed to the within instrument and acknowledged to me that he/she/they executed the same in his/her/their authorized capacity(ies), and that by his/her/their signature(s) on the instrument the person(s), or the entity upon behalf of which the person(s) acted, executed the instrument. WITNESS my hand and official seal.

Signature_____

                              Affiant   _____Known   _____Unknown
                              ID Produced_____
                                                              (Seal)

FICTITIOUS OR ASSUMED NAME CERTIFICATE
BY PARTNERS

CERTIFICATE

The undersigned hereby certify the following:

1.   The undersigned are conducting as   (type of partnership)

partners a business of   (type of business) under the

name of

at:

2.   The real names and the residences of all the partners in said partnership are:

3.   No other person is interested as a partner, part owner, or otherwise in the business

or conduct of it.

This certificate is executed and filed pursuant to state law relating to the conduct of

business under   name.

Dated:

_____
Partner

_____
Partner

STATE OF
COUNTY OF   }

On   before me,   , personally appeared
, personally known to me (or
proved to me on the basis of satisfactory evidence) to be the person(s) whose name(s) is/are
subscribed to the within instrument and acknowledged to me that he/she/they executed the same
in his/her/their authorized capacity(ies), and that by his/her/their signature(s) on the instrument
the person(s), or the entity upon behalf of which the person(s) acted, executed the instrument.
WITNESS my hand and official seal.

Signature_____

Affiant   _____Known   _____Unknown
ID Produced_____
(Seal)

FINAL NOTICE BEFORE LEGAL ACTION

Date:

To:

Dear

    We have repeatedly advised you of your long overdue balance in the amount of

$.

    Since you have not made payment we have turned your account over to our attorneys and instructed them to commence suit without further delay.

    There is still time, however, to avoid suit if you contact us within the next five (5) days.

    This will be your final opportunity to resolve matters without the expense of court proceedings.

Very truly,

_____

FINAL WARNING BEFORE DISMISSAL

Date:

To:

Dear

You have been previously warned of certain problems in your performance as our employee. These problems include:

There has not been a satisfactory improvement in your performance since your last warning. Accordingly, any continued violations of company policy or failure to perform according to the standards of our company shall result in immediate termination of your employment without further warning.

Please contact the undersigned or your supervisor if you have any questions.

Very truly,

_____

GENERAL AGREEMENT

THIS AGREEMENT, made this   day of   , 19   , by and between

(First Party) and   (Second Party).

WITNESSETH: That in consideration of the mutual covenants and agreements to be kept and performed on the part of said parties hereto, respectively as herein stated, the said party of the first part does hereby covenant and agree that it shall:

I.

II.   And said party of the second part covenants and agrees that it shall:

III.   Other terms to be observed by and between the parties:

This agreement shall be binding upon the parties, their successors, assigns and personal representatives. Time is of the essence on all undertakings. This agreement shall be enforced under the laws of the State of   . This is the entire agreement.

Signed the day and year first above written.

Signed in the presence of:

_____   _____
Witness   First Party

_____   _____
Witness   Second Party

GENERAL ASSIGNMENT

BE IT KNOWN, for value received, the undersigned   of

                                        hereby unconditionally and irrevocably assigns and

transfers unto   of   all right, title

and interest in and to the following:

The undersigned fully warrants that it has full rights and authority to enter into this

assignment and that the rights and benefits assigned hereunder are free and clear of any lien,

encumbrance, adverse claim or interest by any third party.

This assignment shall be binding upon and inure to the benefit of the parties, and their

successors and assigns.

Signed this   day of   , 19   .

_____   _____
Witness   Assignor

_____   _____
Witness   Assignee

GENERAL POWER OF ATTORNEY

NOTICE: THIS IS AN IMPORTANT DOCUMENT. BEFORE SIGNING THIS DOCUMENT, YOU SHOULD KNOW THESE IMPORTANT FACTS. THE PURPOSE OF THIS POWER OF ATTORNEY IS TO GIVE THE PERSON WHOM YOU DESIGNATE (YOUR "AGENT") BROAD POWERS TO HANDLE YOUR PROPERTY, WHICH MAY INCLUDE POWERS TO PLEDGE, SELL OR OTHERWISE DISPOSE OF ANY REAL OR PERSONAL PROPERTY WITHOUT ADVANCE NOTICE TO YOU OR APPROVAL BY YOU. YOU MAY SPECIFY THAT THESE POWERS WILL EXIST EVEN AFTER YOU BECOME DISABLED, INCAPACITATED OR INCOMPETENT. THIS DOCUMENT DOES NOT AUTHORIZE ANYONE TO MAKE MEDICAL OR OTHER HEALTH CARE DECISIONS FOR YOU. IF THERE IS ANYTHING ABOUT THIS FORM THAT YOU DO NOT UNDERSTAND, YOU SHOULD ASK A LAWYER TO EXPLAIN IT TO YOU. YOU MAY REVOKE THIS POWER OF ATTORNEY IF YOU LATER WISH TO DO SO.

TO ALL PERSONS, be it known that I,   ,
of   ,
the undersigned Grantor, do hereby make and grant a general power of attorney to
                                                       , of
                                                                          ,
and do thereupon constitute and appoint said individual as my attorney-in-fact.

My attorney-in-fact shall act in my name, place and stead in any way which I myself could do, if I were personally present, with respect to the following matters, to the extent that I am permitted by law to act through an agent:

(**NOTICE**: The Grantor must write his or her initials in the corresponding blank space of a box below with respect to each of the subdivisions (A) through (M) below for which the Grantor wants to give the agent authority. If the blank space within a box for any particular subdivision is NOT initialed, NO AUTHORITY WILL BE GRANTED for matters that are included in that subdivision. Cross out power withheld.

[   ]   (A) Real estate transactions
[   ]   (B) Tangible personal property transactions
[   ]   (C) Bond, share and commodity transactions
[   ]   (D) Banking transactions
[   ]   (E) Business operating transactions
[   ]   (F) Insurance transactions
[   ]   (G) Gifts to charities and individuals other than attorney-in-fact (**If trust distributions are involved or tax consequences are anticipated, consult an attorney.**)
[   ]   (H) Claims and litigation
[   ]   (I) Personal relationships and affairs
[   ]   (J) Benefits from military service
[   ]   (K) Records, reports and statements
[   ]   (L) Full and unqualified authority to my attorney-in-fact to delegate any or all of the foregoing powers to any person or persons whom my attorney-in-fact shall select
[   ]   (M) All other matters

Other Terms:

My attorney-in-fact hereby accepts this appointment subject to its terms and agrees to act and perform in said fiduciary capacity consistent with my best interests as he/she in his/her best discretion deems advisable, and I affirm and ratify all acts so undertaken.

TO INDUCE ANY THIRD PARTY TO ACT HEREUNDER, I HEREBY AGREE THAT ANY THIRD PARTY RECEIVING A DULY EXECUTED COPY OR FACSIMILE OF THIS INSTRUMENT MAY ACT HEREUNDER, AND THAT REVOCATION OR TERMINATION HEREOF SHALL BE INEFFECTIVE AS TO SUCH THIRD PARTY UNLESS AND UNTIL ACTUAL NOTICE OR KNOWLEDGE OF SUCH REVOCATION OR TERMINATION SHALL HAVE BEEN RECEIVED BY SUCH THIRD PARTY, AND I FOR MYSELF AND FOR MY HEIRS, EXECUTORS, LEGAL REPRESENTATIVES AND ASSIGNS, HEREBY AGREE TO INDEMNIFY AND HOLD HARMLESS ANY SUCH THIRD PARTY FROM AND AGAINST ANY AND ALL CLAIMS THAT MAY ARISE AGAINST SUCH THIRD PARTY BY REASON OF SUCH THIRD PARTY HAVING RELIED ON THE PROVISIONS OF THIS INSTRUMENT.

Signed under seal this _____ day of _____ , 19 _____ .

Signed in the presence of:

_____   _____
Witness   Grantor

_____   _____
Witness   Attorney-in-Fact

State of _____ }
County of _____
On _____ before me, _____ ,
appeared _____ ,
personally known to me (or proved to me on the basis of satisfactory evidence) to be the person(s) whose name(s) is/are subscribed to the within instrument and acknowledged to me that he/she/they executed the same in his/her/their authorized capacity(ies), and that by his/her/their signature(s) on the instrument the person(s), or the entity upon behalf of which the person(s) acted, executed the instrument.
WITNESS my hand and official seal.

Signature_____

                                        Affiant _____Known_____Produced ID
                                        Type of ID _____
                                                                            (Seal)

GENERAL RELEASE

FOR GOOD CONSIDERATION, the undersigned jointly and severally hereby forever release, discharge, acquit and forgive _____ from any and all claims, actions, suits, demands, agreements, and each of them, if more than one, liabilities, judgment, and proceedings both at law and in equity arising from the beginning of time to the date of these presents and as more particularly related to or arising from:

This release shall be binding upon and inure to the benefit of the parties, their successors, assigns and personal representatives.

Signed this _____ day of _____ , 19___ .

In the presence of:

_____   _____
Witness   Releasor

                                                                 _____
                                                                 Releasor

GIFT IN ADVANCE OF
TESTAMENTARY BEQUEST

BE IT KNOWN that I,   , of

          , do hereby gift, transfer

and convey to   the below described property

of assets:

It is further acknowledged that this transfer and gift shall be considered an advance against any testamentary bequest I may choose to make to said donee under any trust and/or last will and testament. Said gift has a stipulated value of $ and shall be so deducted from any future testamentary bequest I may make to the donee.

This agreement shall be binding upon and inure to the benefit of the parties, their successors, assigns and personal representatives.

Signed under seal this   day of   , 19   .

In the presence of:

_____   _____

Witness   First Party

_____   _____

Witness   Second Party

STATE OF   }
COUNTY OF

On   before me,   , personally appeared   , personally known to me (or proved to me on the basis of satisfactory evidence) to be the person(s) whose name(s) is/are subscribed to the within instrument and acknowledged to me that he/she/they executed the same in his/her/their authorized capacity(ies), and that by his/her/their signature(s) on the instrument the person(s), or the entity upon behalf of which the person(s) acted, executed the instrument. WITNESS my hand and official seal.

Signature_____

                                Affiant   _____Known   _____Unknown
                                ID Produced_____
                                                     (Seal)

GIFT TO MINOR UNDER UNIFORM GIFT TO MINORS ACT

I, _____ (Donor), of _____

do hereby deliver to _____ of _____ as Custodian

for _____ (Beneficiary) of _____ the following

described property:

This delivery constitutes an unrestricted and irrevocable gift of said property to the Beneficiary under the Uniform Gift to Minors Act of the State of _____ .

The Custodian shall have all manner of right to invest, reinvest, buy, trade, vote, deal with and otherwise exercise all form of powers of the gift property on behalf of the Beneficiary and upon said Beneficiary reaching majority age the Custodian shall deliver said property (or substituted property) with all accrued profits or earnings to said Beneficiary. The Custodian is to serve without bond, or compensation except reimbursement for actual expense.

Signed this _____ day of _____ , 19 ___ .

Witnessed:

_____   _____
Witness   Donor

_____   _____
Witness   Custodian

GRANT OF RIGHT TO USE NAME

In consideration of   dollars
($), payable in the following manner:

The undersigned,   , hereby grants to   ,
as grantee, the sole right to use the name:

for a term of   year(s), commencing on   , 19   , for the

purpose of

The undersigned hereby warrants and guarantees that he or she has not and will not
during said period of this grant give permission or license to use such name for any business
purpose to any other person or entity and that the undersigned will execute all documents and do
all things reasonably requested by grantee to give full effect to this agreement.

Dated: _____
                                                Grantor

                                                _____
                                                Grantee

GUARANTY

FOR GOOD CONSIDERATION, and as an inducement for

_____ (Creditor), from time to time extend credit to _____ (Customer), it is hereby agreed that the undersigned does hereby guaranty to Creditor the prompt, punctual and full payment of all monies now or hereinafter due Creditor from Customer.

Until termination, this guaranty is unlimited as to amount or duration and shall remain in full force and effect notwithstanding any extension, compromise, adjustment, forbearance, waiver, release or discharge of any party obligor or guarantor, or release in whole or in part of any security granted for said indebtedness or compromise or adjustment thereto, and the undersigned waives all notices thereto.

The obligations of the undersigned shall at the election of Creditor be primary and not necessarily secondary and Creditor shall not be required to exhaust its remedies as against Customer prior to enforcing its rights under this guaranty against the undersigned.

The guaranty hereunder shall be unconditional and absolute and the undersigned waive all rights of subrogation and set-off until all sums due under this guaranty are fully paid. The undersigned further waives all suretyship defenses or defenses in the nature thereof, generally.

In the event payments due under this guaranty are not punctually paid upon demand, then the undersigned shall pay all reasonable costs and attorney's fees necessary for collection, and enforcement of this guaranty.

If there are two or more guarantors to this guaranty, the obligations shall be joint and several and binding upon and inure to the benefit of the parties, their successors, assigns and personal representatives.

This guaranty may be terminated by any guarantor upon fifteen (15) days written notice of termination, mailed certified mail, return receipt requested to the Creditor. Such termination shall extend only to credit extended beyond said fifteen (15) day period and not to prior extended credit, or goods in transit received by Customer beyond said date, or for special orders placed prior to said date notwithstanding date of delivery. Termination of this guaranty by any guarantor shall not impair the continuing guaranty of any remaining guarantors of said termination.

Each of the undersigned warrants and represents it has full authority to enter into this guaranty.

This guaranty shall be binding upon and inure to the benefit of the parties, their successors, assigns and personal representatives.

This guaranty shall be construed and enforced under the laws of the state of

.

Signed this   day of   , 19   .

In the presence of:

_____   _____
Witness   Guarantor

_____   _____
Witness   Guarantor

GUARANTY OF RENTS

FOR GOOD CONSIDERATION and as an inducement for

of _____ (Landlord) to enter into a lease or tenancy

agreement with _____ of _____

(Tenant) for premises at

BE IT KNOWN, that the Undersigned do hereby jointly and severally guaranty to the Landlord and his successors and assigns the prompt, punctual and full payment of all rents and other charges that may become due and owing from Tenant to Landlord under said lease or tenancy agreement or any renewal or extension thereof. This guaranty shall also extend or apply to any damages incurred by Landlord for any breach of lease in addition to the failure to pay rents or other charges due under the lease.

Signed this _____ day of _____ , 19 ____ .

Witnessed:

_____   _____
Witness   Guarantor

_____   _____
Witness   Guarantor

INCUMBENCY CERTIFICATE

I, _____ , Secretary of

do hereby affirm and verify that the duly constituted officers of the Corporation as of

_____ , 19____ , are:

_____ , President

_____ , Vice President

_____ , Treasurer

_____ , Secretary

A True Record:

Attest:

_____
Secretary

STATE OF _____ }
COUNTY OF _____ }

On _____ before me, _____ , personally appeared
_____ , personally known to me (or
proved to me on the basis of satisfactory evidence) to be the person(s) whose name(s) is/are
subscribed to the within instrument and acknowledged to me that he/she/they executed the same
in his/her/their authorized capacity(ies), and that by his/her/their signature(s) on the instrument
the person(s), or the entity upon behalf of which the person(s) acted, executed the instrument.
WITNESS my hand and official seal.

Signature_____

Affiant _____Known _____Unknown
ID Produced_____
(Seal)

INDEMNITY AGREEMENT

FOR VALUE RECEIVED, the undersigned jointly and severally agree to indemnify and save harmless _____ (Indemnities) and their successors and assigns, from any claim, action, liability, loss, damage or suit, arising from the following:

In the event of any asserted claim, the Indemnities shall provide the undersigned reasonably timely written notice of same, and thereafter the undersigned shall at its own expense defend, protect and save harmless Indemnities against said claim or any loss or liability thereunder.

In the further event the undersigned shall fail to so defend and/or indemnify and save harmless, then in such instance the Indemnities shall have full rights to defend, pay or settle said claim on their own behalf without notice to undersigned and with full rights to recourse against the undersigned for all fees, costs, expenses and payments made or agreed to be paid to discharge said claim.

Upon default, the undersigned further agree to pay all reasonable attorney's fees necessary to enforce this agreement.

This agreement shall be unlimited as to amount or duration.

This agreement shall be binding upon and inure to the benefit of the parties, their successors, assigns and personal representatives.

Signed this _____ day of _____ , 19 __ .

Witnessed:

_____   _____
Witness   First Party

_____   _____
Witness   Second Party

INDEPENDENT CONTRACTOR AGREEMENT

Agreement is made this   day of   , 19   .

The following outlines our agreement:

You have been retained by   , as an independent contractor for the project of

You will be responsible for successfully completing said project according to specifications.

The project is to be completed by   .

The cost to complete will not exceed $.

You will invoice us for your services rendered at the end of each month.

We will not deduct or withhold any taxes, FICA or other deductions. As an independent contractor, you will not be entitled to any fringe benefits, such as unemployment insurance, medical insurance, pension plans, or other such benefits that would be offered to regular employees.

During this project you may be in contact with or directly working with proprietary information which is important to our company and its competitive position. All information must be treated with strict confidence and may not be used at any time or in any manner in work you may do with others in our industry.

Agreed:

Independent Contractor_____ Date_____

Company Representative_____ Date_____

INDIVIDUAL ACKNOWLEDGEMENT

STATE OF

COUNTY OF   }

On the   day of   , 19 , before me personally appeared   ,
to me known to be the individual described in and who executed the document annexed hereto
and who executed same in my presence or acknowledged said signature as a true and free act
and deed, before me.

On   before me,   , personally appeared
                          , personally known to me (or
proved to me on the basis of satisfactory evidence) to be the person(s) whose name(s) is/are
subscribed to the within instrument and acknowledged to me that he/she/they executed the same
in his/her/their authorized capacity(ies), and that by his/her/their signature(s) on the instrument
the person(s), or the entity upon behalf of which the person(s) acted, executed the instrument.
WITNESS my hand and official seal.

Signature_____

                                    Affiant   _____Known   _____Unknown
                                    ID Produced_____
                                                              (Seal)

INFORMATION REQUEST ON DISPUTED CHARGE

Date:

To:

Dear

   Please be advised that we have received your statement of charges and we dispute certain charges on our account for the following reasons:

   We do want to promptly reconcile our account, so we may pay and resolve this matter; however, we find we need the below checked information or documents:

   _____   Copies of charges noted on reverse side

   _____   Copies of purchase orders

   _____   Debit memoranda outstanding

   _____   List of goods claimed as shipped

   _____   Other:

Thank you for your immediate attention. Upon receipt of the requested information we shall give your statement our prompt consideration.

Very truly,

_____

INSURANCE CLAIM NOTICE

Date:

To:

Dear

    You are hereby notified that we have incurred a loss covered by insurance you underwrite. The claim information is as follows:

    1.   Type of Loss or Claim:

    2.   Date and Time Incurred:

    3.   Location:

    4.   Estimated Loss or Casualty:

Please forward a claim form or have an adjuster call me at the below telephone number.

            Very truly,

_____   _____

Policy Number   Name

                         _____

                         Address

                         _____

_____   _____

Telephone No. (Work)   Telephone No. (Home)

INVITATION TO QUOTE PRICE OF GOODS

Date:

To:

Please quote your ordinary unit price for supplying the following goods together with your discount for volume purchases:

Please also indicate:

(a)   whether your quotes are inclusive or exclusive of sales taxes; if not otherwise stated, we will assume your quotes are inclusive of sales taxes;

(b)   delivery time from receipt of our purchase order to receipt of your shipment;

(c)   if delivery costs are not included in your quote, please state this clearly, otherwise we will assume they are included; if delivery is included, please state the price of goods if we pick up;

(d)   your terms of payment.

All price quotations must be firm and state when they expire.

Very truly,

_____

IRREVOCABLE PROXY

I, _____ , the holder of _____ shares of the

common voting stock of _____

Corporation, do hereby irrevocably appoint _____

as my proxy to attend the shareholder's meeting of _____

Corporation, to be held on _____ , 19 ___ , or any continuations or adjournments

of that meeting, with full power to vote and act for me and in my name and place, in the same

manner, and to the same extent that I might act if I would have been in attendance at such

meeting.

This proxy is irrevocable and has been issued to _____ ,

who is a pledgee holding a valid pledge of the shares owned by me. Any other proxy or proxies

previously given by me to others is hereby revoked.

Date: _____

_____

STATE OF _____ }
COUNTY OF _____ }

On _____ before me, _____ , personally appeared
_____ , personally known to me (or
proved to me on the basis of satisfactory evidence) to be the person(s) whose name(s) is/are
subscribed to the within instrument and acknowledged to me that he/she/they executed the same
in his/her/their authorized capacity(ies), and that by his/her/their signature(s) on the instrument
the person(s), or the entity upon behalf of which the person(s) acted, executed the instrument.
WITNESS my hand and official seal.

Signature_____

Affiant _____Known _____Unknown
ID Produced_____
(Seal)

LANDLORD'S AND TENANT'S MUTUAL RELEASE

BE IT KNOWN, that _____ of _____
(Landlord) hereby acknowledges that _____ of _____
_____ (Tenant) duly delivered up possession of the premises known as

_____

and Tenant has fully paid all rents due and performed all obligations under said tenancy.

And Tenant acknowledges surrender of said premises as of this date and acknowledges return of any security deposit due from Landlord.

Now, therefore, Landlord and Tenant release and discharge one and the other and their successors and assigns from any and all claims arising under said tenancy.

Signed this _____ day of _____ , 19 _____ .

In the presence of:

_____   _____
Witness   Landlord

_____   _____
Witness   Tenant

LANDLORD'S NOTICE TO TERMINATE TENANCY

Date:

To:

Please be advised that as your landlord you are hereby notified that we intend to terminate your tenancy on the premises you now occupy as our tenant, said premises are described as:

Your tenancy shall be terminated on   , 19   . We shall require that you deliver to us full possession of the rented premises on said date, free of all your goods and possessions together, we also request all keys to the premises.

Upon your full compliance, and if applicable, we shall thereupon return any security deposit or escrow we may be holding and that may be due you. Rent for the premises is due and payable through and including the termination date.

Thank you for your cooperation.

_____
Landlord

_____
Address

_____

CERTIFIED MAIL, Return Receipt Requested

LANDLORD'S NOTICE TO VACATE

Date:

To:

To the above Tenant and all others now in possession of the below described premises:

You are hereby requested to quit, vacate and deliver possession thereof to the undersigned on or before _____ , 19 .

This notice to vacate is due to your following breach of tenancy:

Should you fail, refuse or neglect to pay your rent, cure the breach, or vacate said premises within _____ days from service of this notice, I will take such legal action as the law requires to evict you from the premises. You are to further understand that we shall in all instances hold you responsible for all present and future rents due under your tenancy agreement.

Thank you for your cooperation.

_____

CERTIFIED MAIL, Return Receipt Requested

LAST WILL AND TESTAMENT OF

_____

BE IT KNOWN, that I, _____of
_____, County of _____,
in the State of _____ being of sound mind, do make
and declare this to be my Last Will and Testament expressly revoking all my prior Wills and
Codicils at any time made.

I. PERSONAL REPRESENTATIVE:

I appoint   of
                          , as Personal Representative of this my Last Will and Testament and
provide if this Personal Representative is unable or unwilling to serve then I appoint
                                              of   , as alternate Personal
Representative. My Personal Representative shall be authorized to carry out all provisions of this
Will and pay my just debts, obligations and funeral expenses. I further provide my Personal
Representative shall not be required to post surety bond in this or any other jurisdiction, and
direct that no expert appraisal be made of my estate unless required by law.

II. GUARDIAN:

In the event I shall die as the sole parent of minor children, then I appoint
                                         , as Guardian of said minor children. If this named
Guardian is unable or unwilling to serve, then I appoint
as alternate Guardian.

III. BEQUESTS:

I direct that after payment of all my just debts, my property be bequeathed in the
manner following:

_____
Testator Initials

Page ____ of ____.

Execute and attest before a notary.

NOTE: If your gross estate exceeds $600,000 ($1,200,000 for a married couple), consult an attorney.
CAUTION: Louisiana residents should consult an attorney before preparing a will.

IN WITNESS WHEREOF, I have hereunto set my hand this _____ day of _____ , 19 ____ , to this my Last Will and Testament.

_____
Testator Signature

IV.   WITNESSED:

The testator has signed this will at the end and on each other separate page, and has declared or signified in our presence that it is his/her last will and testament, and in the presence of the testator and each other we have hereunto subscribed our names this _____ day of _____ , 19 ____ .

_____   _____
Witness Signature   Address

_____   _____
Witness Signature   Address

_____   _____
Witness Signature   Address

State of _____
County of _____ }

We, _____ , _____ ,

_____ , and _____ ,
the testator and the witnesses, respectively, whose names are signed to the attached and foregoing instrument, were sworn and declared to the undersigned that the testator signed the instrument as his/her Last Will and that each of the witnesses, in the presence of the testator and each other, signed the will as a witness.

Testator: _____   Witness _____

                                                Witness _____

                                                Witness _____

On _____ before me, _____ ,
appeared
personally known to me (or proved to me on the basis of satisfactory evidence) to be the person(s) whose name(s) is/are subscribed to the within instrument and acknowledged to me that he/she/they executed the same in his/her/their authorized capacity(ies), and that by his/her/their signature(s) on the instrument the person(s), or the entity upon behalf of which the person(s) acted, executed the instrument.
WITNESS my hand and official seal.

Signature_____

                              Affiant _____ Known_____Produced ID
                              Type of ID_____

                                                          (Seal)

Page ____ of ____.

LEASE TERMINATION AGREEMENT

FOR GOOD CONSIDERATION, be it acknowledged that   of   (Lessee) and

of   (Lessor) under a certain lease agreement between the parties dated   , 19   , (Lease), do hereby mutually agree to terminate and cancel said Lease effective   , 19   . All rights and obligations under said Lease shall thereupon be cancelled excepting only for any rents under the Lease accruing prior to the effective termination date which then remain unpaid or otherwise not satisfied, and which shall be paid by Lessee on or prior to the termination date.

Lessee agrees to promptly surrender the premises to Lessor on or before the termination date and deliver same to Lessor in good condition free of the Lessee's goods and effects, waiving all further rights to possession.

This agreement shall be binding upon the parties, their successors, assigns and personal representatives.

Signed this   day of   , 19   .

In the presence of:

_____   _____
Witness   Lessee

_____   _____
Witness   Lessor

LETTER REQUESTING AUTHORIZATION
TO RELEASE CREDIT INFORMATION

Thank you for your recent interest in establishing credit with our company. Please sign the authorization to release credit information below and complete the enclosed form. Then submit it to us with your most recent financial statements. We will contact your credit and bank references and then contact you regarding credit with our company.

Thank you,

Credit Manager

The undersigned has recently applied for credit with   .
The undersigned has been requested to provide information concerning my credit history. Therefore, I authorize the investigation of my credit information.

The release by you of information is authorized whether such information is of record or not. I do hereby release you and all persons, agencies, agents, employees, firms, companies, or parties affiliated with you from any damages resulting from providing such information.

This authorization is valid for thirty (30) days from the date of my signature below. Please keep a copy of my release request for your files.

Thank you for your cooperation.

Signature _____ Date _____

LIMITED GUARANTY

BE IT KNOWN, for good consideration, and as an inducement for

(Creditor) to extend credit from time to time to

(Customer) the undersigned jointly, severally and unconditionally guarantee to Creditor the prompt and punctual payment of certain sums now or hereinafter due Creditor from Customer, provided that the liability of the guarantors hereunder, whether singularly or collectively, shall be limited to the sum of $ as a maximum liability and guarantors shall not be liable under this guarantee for any greater or further amount.

The undersigned guarantors agree to remain fully bound on this guarantee, notwithstanding any extension, forbearance, indulgence or waiver, or release or discharge or substitution of any party or collateral or security for the debt. In the event of default, Creditor may seek payment directly from the undersigned without need to proceed first against borrower. Guarantors further waive all suretyship defenses consistent with this limited guaranty. In the event of default, the guarantor shall be responsible for all attorneys' fees and reasonable costs of collection, which may be in addition to the limited guaranty amount.

This guaranty shall be binding upon and inure to the benefit of the parties, their successors, assigns and personal representatives.

Signed this   day of   , 19   .

In the presence of:

_____   _____
Witness   Guarantor

_____   _____
Witness   Guarantor

LOST CREDIT CARD NOTICE

Date:

To:

Dear

     Please be advised that the below described credit card has been lost or stolen. You are therefore requested to stop issuance of further credit against said card until notified to the contrary by the undersigned.

     Please notify me at once if charges appeared against said card after   ,
19 , as this was the date the card was lost or stolen and subsequent charges were unauthorized.

     Please send me a replacement card.

     Thank you for your cooperation.

Very truly,

_____

Cardholder

_____

Address

_____

Credit Card Number

CERTIFIED MAIL, Return Receipt Requested

MAILING LIST NAME REMOVAL REQUEST

Date:

To:

Dear

      Please be advised that I have received unsolicited mail from your firm. I hereby request that you remove my name from your mailing list, and that you not send me unsolicited material in the future.

      My name and address appears as below (or as per mailing label attached).

_____

Name

_____

Street Address

_____

City, State

Thank you for your attention to this request.

Very truly,

_____

MINUTES, FIRST MEETING
OF SHAREHOLDERS

The first meeting of the shareholders of

was held at   on the   day of

, 19   , at   o'clock   .m.

The meeting was duly called and held by order of the President. The President stated the purpose of the meeting.

Next, the Secretary read the list of shareholders as they appear in the record book of the Corporation, and noted that the required quorum of shareholders were present.

Next, the Secretary read a waiver of notice of the meeting, signed by all shareholders. On a motion duly made, seconded and carried, the waiver was ordered attached to the minutes of this meeting.

Next, the President asked the Secretary to read: (1) the minutes of the organization meeting of the Corporation; and (2) the minutes of the first meeting of the Board of Directors.

A motion was duly made, seconded and carried unanimously that the following resolution be adopted:

WHEREAS, the minutes of the organization meeting of the Corporation and the minutes of the first meeting of the Board of Directors have been read to this meeting, and

WHEREAS, bylaws were adopted and directors and officers were elected at the organization meeting, it is hereby

RESOLVED that this meeting approves and ratifies the election of the said directors and officers of this Corporation for the term of   years and approves, ratifies and adopts said bylaws as the bylaws of the corporation. It is further

RESOLVED that all acts taken and decisions made at the organization meeting and the first meeting of the Board are approved and ratified. It is further

RESOLVED that signing of these minutes constitutes full ratification by the signatories and waiver of notice of the meeting.

There being no further business, it was voted to adjourn the meeting, dated this

day of   , 19   .

_____
Secretary

_____

_____

_____

_____

Directors

Appended hereto:

    Waiver of notice of meeting.

MINUTES OF COMBINED MEETING
OF STOCKHOLDERS AND DIRECTORS

A combined meeting of Stockholders and Directors was held at the office of the Corporation, at _____ on _____ , 19___ , at ___ .m.

The following Directors were present at the meeting:

_____	_____
_____	_____
_____	_____

being a quorum of the Directors of the Corporation.

The following Shareholders were present in person or by proxy at the meeting:

_____	_____
_____	_____
_____	_____

being a quorum of the Shareholders of the Corporation.

_____ , President of the Corporation, chaired the meeting, and _____ , Secretary of the Corporation, acted as secretary of the meeting.

The Secretary presented notice or waiver of notice of the meeting, signed by all interested parties.

The meeting, having been duly convened, was ready to proceed with its business, whereupon it was:

The Secretary announced that _____ shares of common stock had been voted in favor of the foregoing resolution(s) and _____ shares of common stock had been voted against the resolution(s), said vote representing more than _____ % of the outstanding shares entitled to vote thereon.

The President thereupon declared that the resolution(s) had been duly adopted.

There being no further business, upon motion, the meeting was adjourned.

_____
Secretary

MINUTES OF DIRECTORS' MEETING

A regular meeting of the Board of Directors of
was duly called and held on   , 19   , at
        commencing at   o'clock   .m.   There were present and participating
at the meeting:

With approval of the directors present,   acted as Chair of the
meeting and   recorded the minutes.

On motions duly made and seconded, it was voted that:

1.   The minutes of the last meeting of directors be taken as read.

2.   That it be further VOTED:

There being no further business, the meeting was adjourned.

Date:

_____
Secretary

MINUTES OF SPECIAL MEETING OF STOCKHOLDERS

_____

A special meeting of the stockholders of the above Corporation was duly called and held at   , in the City of   , in the State of   , on   , 19   , at   o'clock   .m.

The meeting was called to order by   , the President of the Corporation, and   , the Secretary of the Corporation, kept the records of the meeting and its proceedings.

The Secretary noted that a quorum of stockholders were present in person or were represented by proxy, the aggregate amount representing more than   % of the outstanding stock entitled to vote on the resolutions proposed at the meeting.

The Secretary reported that the following stockholders were present in person:

Names	Number of Shares
_____	_____
_____	_____
_____	_____

and that the following stockholders were represented by proxy:

Names	Names of Proxies	Number of Shares
_____	_____	_____
_____	_____	_____
_____	_____	_____

The Secretary presented and read a waiver of notice of the meeting signed by each stockholder entitled to notice of the meeting, said waiver of notice was ordered to be filed with the minutes of the meeting.

On motion duly made and seconded, and after due deliberation, the following resolution(s) was/were voted upon:

The Secretary reported that   shares of common stock had been voted in favor of the foregoing resolution(s) and   shares of common stock had been voted against the resolutions, said vote representing more than   % of the outstanding shares entitled to vote thereon.

The President thereupon declared that the resolution(s) had been duly adopted.

There being no further business, upon motion, the meeting adjourned.

A True Record

Attest

_____

Secretary

MORTGAGE BOND

KNOW ALL MEN BY THESE PRESENTS, that

(Obligor) does hereby acknowledge that Obligor is indebted to   ,

having an office at

County of   , State of   (Obligee), in the principal

sum of   dollars

($), which sum with interest on the unpaid balances to be computed from the date

hereof at the rate of   percent (%) per annum, Obligor does covenant to pay to

Obligee, at the office of Obligee in   , or such other

place as Obligee may designate in writing,   dollars ($) on the first day

of   , 19   , and thereafter in   payments of   dollars

($) on the first day of each subsequent month, until the principal and interest are fully

paid, except that the final payment of the entire indebtedness evidenced hereby, shall be due and

payable on the first of   , 19   .

The whole or any part of the principal sum and of any other sums of money secured by

the mortgage given to secure this Bond shall, at the option of Obligee, become due and payable

if default be made in any payment under this Bond or upon the happening of any default that, by

the terms of the mortgage given to secure this Bond, shall entitle the mortgagee to declare the

principal sum, or any part thereof, to be due and payable; and all the covenants, agreements,

terms, and conditions of the mortgage are incorporated in this Bond with the same force and

effect as if set forth at length.

If more than one person joins in the execution of this Bond, the relative words herein

shall be read as if written in the plural, and the words "Obligor" and "Obligee" shall include

their heirs, executors, administrators, successors and assigns.

Signed this   day of   , 19   .

_____

Obligor

MORTGAGE DEED

This Mortgage is given by   , hereinafter called Borrower, of

to   , hereinafter called Lender, which term includes any holder of this Mortgage, to secure the payment of the PRINCIPAL SUM of $ together with interest thereon computed on the outstanding balance, all as provided in a Note having the same date as this Mortgage, and also to secure the performance of all the terms, covenants, agreements, conditions and extensions of the Note and this Mortgage.

In consideration of the loan made by Lender to Borrower and for the purpose expressed above, the Borrower does hereby grant and convey to Lender, with MORTGAGE COVENANTS, thc land with the buildings situated thereon and all the improvements and fixtures now and hereafter a part thereof, being more particularly described in Exhibit A attached hereto and made a part hereof and having a street address of:

Attach Property Description

Borrower further covenants and agrees that:

1. No superior mortgage or the note secured by it will be modified without the consent of Lender hereunder.

2. Borrower will make with each periodic payment due under the Note secured by this Mortgage a payment sufficient to provide a fund from which the real estate taxes, betterment assessments and other municipal charges which can become a lien against the mortgaged premises can be paid by Lender when due. This provision shall be effective only in the event that a fund for the same purpose is not required to be established by the holder of a senior mortgage.

3. In the event that Borrower fails to carry out the covenants and agreements set forth herein, the Lender may do and pay for whatever is necessary to protect the value of and the Lender's rights in the mortgaged property and any amounts so paid shall be added to the Principal Sum due the Lender hereunder.

4. As additional security hereunder, Borrower hereby assigns to Lender, Borrower's rents of the mortgaged property, and upon default the same may be collected without the necessity of making entry upon the mortgaged premises.

5. In the event that any condition of this Mortgage or any senior mortgage shall be in default for fifteen (15) days, the entire debt shall become immediately due and payable at the option of the Lender. Lender shall be entitled to collect all costs and expenses, including reasonable attorney's fees incurred.

6. In the event that the Borrower transfers ownership (either legal or equitable) or any security interest in the mortgaged property, whether voluntarily or involuntarily, the Lender may at its option declare the entire debt due and payable.

7. This Mortgage is also security for all other direct and contingent liabilities of the Borrower to Lender which are due or become due and whether now existing or hereafter contracted.

8. Borrower shall maintain adequate insurance on the property in amounts and form of coverage acceptable to Lender and the Lender shall be a named insured as its interest may appear.

9. Borrower shall not commit waste or permit others to commit actual, permissive or constructive waste on the property.

10. Borrower further covenants and warrants to Lender that Borrower is indefeasibly seized of said land in fee simple; that the Borrower has lawful authority to mortgage said land and that said land is free and clear of all encumbrances except as may be expressly contained herein.

This Mortgage is upon the STATUTORY CONDITION and the other conditions set forth herein, for breach of which Lender shall have the STATUTORY POWER OF SALE to the extent existing under State law.

Executed under seal this   day of   , 19   .

_____   _____
Borrower   Borrower

STATE OF
COUNTY OF   }

On   before me,   , personally appeared
                                                  , personally known to me (or proved to me on the basis of satisfactory evidence) to be the person(s) whose name(s) is/are subscribed to the within instrument and acknowledged to me that he/she/they executed the same in his/her/their authorized capacity(ies), and that by his/her/their signature(s) on the instrument the person(s), or the entity upon behalf of which the person(s) acted, executed the instrument. WITNESS my hand and official seal.

Signature_____

                                    Affiant   _____Known   _____Unknown
                                    ID Produced_____
                                                            (Seal)

MUTUAL CANCELLATION OF CONTRACT

BE IT KNOWN, that for value received, that the undersigned

and   being parties to a certain contract dated   ,

19   , whereas said contract provides for:

do hereby mutually cancel and terminate said contract, effective this date.

We further provide that said termination shall be without further recourse by either party against the other and this document shall constitute mutual releases of any further obligations under said contract, all to the same extent as if said contract had not been entered into in the first instance, provided the parties shall herewith undertake the below described acts to terminate said contract, which obligations, if any, shall remain binding, notwithstanding this agreement to cancel.

Signed this   day of   , 19   .

In the presence of:

_____   _____
Witness   First Party

_____   _____
Witness   Second Party

MUTUAL RELEASES

BE IT KNOWN, for good consideration, and in further consideration of the mutual releases herein entered into, that:

(First Party) and

(Second Party) do hereby completely, mutually and reciprocally release, discharge, acquit and forgive each other from all claims, contracts, actions, suits, demands, agreements, liabilities, and proceedings of every nature and description both at law and in equity that either party has or may have against the other, arising from the beginning of time to the date of these presence, including but not necessarily limited to an incident or claim described as:

This release shall be binding upon and inure to the benefit of the parties, their successors, assigns and personal representatives.

Signed this   day of   , 19   .

In the presence of:

_____   _____
Witness   First Party

_____   _____
Witness   Second Party

NON-COMPETE AGREEMENT

FOR GOOD CONSIDERATION, the undersigned jointly and severally covenant and agree not to compete with the business of   (Company) and its lawful successors and assigns.

The term "non compete" as used herein shall mean that the Undersigned shall not directly or indirectly engage in a business or other activity described as:

notwithstanding whether said participation be as an owner, officer, director, employee, agent, consultant, partner or stockholder (excepting as a passive investment in a publicly owned company).

This covenant shall extend only for a radius of   miles from the present location of the Company at   and shall remain in full force and effect for   years from date hereof.

In the event of any breach, the Company shall be entitled to full injunctive relief without need to post bond, which rights shall be cumulative with and not necessarily successive or exclusive of any other legal rights.

This agreement shall be binding upon and inure to the benefit of the parties, their successors, assigns and personal representatives.

Signed this   day of   , 19   .

Witnessed:

_____   _____
Witness   First Party

_____   _____
Witness   Second Party

NONDISCLOSURE AGREEMENT

To induce _____ (Client) to retain _____ (Promisor) as an outside consultant and to furnish Promisor with certain information that is proprietary and confidential, Promisor hereby warrants, represents, covenants, and agrees as follows:

1.   Engagement. Promisor, in the course of engagement by Client, may or will have access to or learn certain information belonging to Client that is proprietary and confidential (Confidential Information).

2.   Definition of Confidential Information. Confidential Information as used throughout this Agreement means any secret or proprietary information relating directly to Client's business and that of Client's affiliated companies and subsidiaries, including, but not limited to, products, customer lists, pricing policies, employment records and policies, operational methods, marketing plans and strategies, product development techniques or plans, business acquisition plans, new personnel acquisition plans, methods of manufacture, technical processes, designs and design projects, inventions and research programs, trade "know-how," trade secrets, specific software, algorithms, computer processing systems, object and source codes, user manuals, systems documentation, and other business affairs of Client and its affiliated companies and subsidiaries.

3.   Nondisclosure. Promisor agrees to keep strictly confidential all Confidential Information and will not, without Client's express written authorization, signed by one of Client's authorized officers, use, sell, market, or disclose any Confidential Information to any third person, firm, corporation, or association for any purpose. Promisor further agrees not to make any copies of the Confidential Information except upon Client's written authorization, signed by one of Client's authorized officers, and will not remove any copy or sample of Confidential Information from the premises of Client without such authorization.

4.   Return of Material. Upon receipt of a written request from Client, Promisor will return to Client all copies or samples of Confidential Information that, at the time of the receipt of the notice, are in Promisor's possession.

5.   Obligations Continue Past Term. The obligations imposed on Promisor shall continue with respect to each unit of the Confidential Information following the termination of the business relationship between Promisor and Client, and such obligations shall not terminate until such unit shall cease to be secret and confidential and shall be in the public domain, unless such event shall have occurred as a result of wrongful conduct by Promisor or Promisor's agents, servants, officers, or employees or a breach of the covenants set forth in this Agreement.

6.   Equitable Relief. Promisor acknowledges and agrees that a breach of the provisions of Paragraph 3 or 4 of this Agreement would cause Client to suffer irreparable damage that could not be adequately remedied by an action at law. Accordingly, Promisor agrees that Client shall have the right to seek specific performance of the provisions of Paragraph 3 to enjoin a breach or attempted breach of the provision thereof, such right being in addition to all other rights and remedies that are available to Client at law, in equity, or otherwise.

7.   Invalidity. If any provision of this Agreement or its application is held to be invalid, illegal, or unenforceable in any respect, the validity, legality, or enforceability of any of the other provisions and applications therein shall not in any way be affected or impaired.

IN WITNESS WHEREOF, this Agreement has been signed on the _____ day of _____ , 19____ .

_____   _____
Witness   Promisor

NOTICE OF ASSIGNMENT

Date:

To:

Dear

You are hereby notified that on   , 19   , we have assigned and

transferred to   the following

existing between us:

Please direct any further correspondence (or payments, if applicable) to them at the

following address:

_____

_____

_____

Please contact us should you have any questions, and we thank you for your cooperation.

Very truly,

_____

NOTICE OF ASSIGNMENT TO OBLIGOR

Date:

To:

Dear

    Please take notice of the attached assignment, and hold all sums of money affected by such assignment, now or hereafter in your possession, that otherwise are payable to me, for the benefit of   , assignee, in accordance with the provisions of said assignment, the terms of our original agreement.

    An authenticated copy of this assignment was filed by me on   , 19   , in the office of the   .

                                Very truly,

_____

NOTICE OF CHANGE IN RENT

Date:

To:

Dear

     Please be advised that effective   , 19   , the monthly rent for the rented premises you now occupy as my Tenant at   shall be increased to $ per month, payable in advance on the   day of each month during your continued tenancy. This is a change from your present rent of $ per month.

     All other terms of your tenancy shall remain as presently in effect.

                                 Very truly,

                         _____

                         Landlord

NOTICE OF C.O.D. TERMS

Date:

To:

Dear

      We are in receipt of your order dated   , 19   , and your request for credit terms.

      While we do want to accept your order, we regret we cannot ship on credit terms at the present time, due to inadequate credit.

      Accordingly, we propose shipment on C.O.D. terms. We will assume C.O.D. terms are satisfactory to you unless we are notified of the contrary within ten (10) days.

      Thank you for your understanding and we appreciate your patronage, with the hope we may more favorably consider credit requests in the future.

Very truly,

_____

NOTICE OF DEBT ASSIGNMENT

Date:

To:

    Re: Balance Due $

Dear

    Reference is made to a certain debt or obligation due from you to the above captioned party.

    On   , 19   , all rights to receive future payment have been assigned to the undersigned. A copy of the assignment is attached. We understand the balance due is $.

    Accordingly, we provide you notice of said assignment and direct that all future payments on said account be directed to the undersigned at the below address. Further, checks should be made payable to the undersigned.

    It is important that all payments be made as directed to insure credit. You understand this is not a dunning notice or a reflection on your credit.

    We appreciate your cooperation.

                Very truly,

                _____

NOTICE OF DEFAULT BY ASSIGNEE TO OBLIGOR

Date:

To:

      Please take notice that you are in default in the amount of

dollars ($), having failed to make the following payments due to me on the

indebtedness of   dollars ($),

described in and secured by an assignment, dated   , 19   , made by

          , assignor, to me and filed on   , 19 , in

County Clerk's Office, filing No.   , and notice of which assignment was

served on you on   , 19 . The payments that you are in default are the

following:

      Unless such amounts or such payment thereon as I may accept are made within

days from the date of mailing of this notice, I will sue to collect.

                                            _____

NOTICE OF DEFAULT IN PAYMENT

Date:

To:

You are hereby notified that your payment of

Dollars ($) due on or before   , has not been received

by the undersigned. If said payment is not paid by   , the undersigned

shall invoke the remedies under the agreement between us dated   , together

with such other remedies that the undersigned may have.

_____

NOTICE OF DEFAULT ON PROMISSORY NOTE

Date:

To:

Dear

    We refer to your promissory note dated   , 19   , in the original principal amount of $ and to which we, the undersigned, are holder.

    Notice is hereby provided that you are in default under said note in that the following payment(s) have not been received.

Payment Due Date	Amount Due

| | _____ |
| Total Arrears | $ |

    Accordingly, demand is hereby made for full payment of the entire balance of $ due under the note. If payment is not received within   days, this note shall be forwarded to our attorneys for collection and you shall additionally be liable for all reasonable cost of collection, and accrued interest and late charges.

                    Very truly,

_____

NOTICE OF DISMISSAL

Date:

To:

We regret to notify you that your employment with the firm shall be terminated on
_____, 19____, because of the following reasons:

_____

_____

_____

_____

_____

Severance pay shall be in accordance with company policy. Within 30 days of termination we shall issue to you a statement of accrued benefits. Any insurance benefits shall continue in accordance with applicable law and/or the provisions of our personnel policy. Please contact _____, at your earliest convenience, who will explain each of these items and arrange with you for the return of any company property.

We sincerely regret this action is necessary.

Very truly,

_____

Copies to:

NOTICE OF DISPUTED ACCOUNT

Date:

To:

Dear

      We refer to your Invoice or Statement No.   , dated   , 19   , in the amount of $.

      We dispute the balance claimed for the following reason(s):

_____   Items billed for have not been received.

_____   Prices are in excess of agreed amount. Credit of $ is claimed.

_____   Prior payment made in the amount of $ made on   , 19   , was not credited.

_____   Goods were unordered, and are available for return on shipping instructions.

_____   Goods were defective as per prior notice.

_____   Goods are available for return and credit per sales items.

_____   Other:

      Therefore, we request you promptly credit our account in the amount of $ so that this account may be satisfactorily cleared.

                        Very truly,

                     _____

NOTICE OF ELECTION TO CANCEL

Date:

To:

     You are hereby notified that   has elected to cancel and terminate, and cancels and terminates, effective   , 19 , the following written contract entered into with you, all in accordance with the terms and provisions of the contract:

_____

NOTICE OF FORFEITURE

Date:

To:

Please take notice that the undersigned elects to declare the agreement forfeited and void that was executed by you and the undersigned on   , 19   , for the reason that you have failed to abide by the terms of the agreement in the following manner:

_____

NOTICE OF INTENT TO REPOSSESS DUE TO DEFAULT

Date:

To:

You are in default under a certain lease contract dated   for the following reason(s):

This letter serves as notice to you of said default. It is also notice to you that, unless you communicate with the undersigned within   days from the date of this letter, we shall exercise our rights upon default as stated in the lease contract, including our right to take immediate possession of the following leased item(s):

Very truly,

_____

NOTICE OF LEASE

The undersigned Lessor and Lessee do hereby provide public notice of the following lease:

1. Lessor:

2. Lessee:

3. Leased Premises:

4. Term of Lease is   years commencing on   , 19   and ending on   , 19   .

5. Options to Extend Lease:

6. Option to Acquire Property or Right of First Refusal:

_____
Lessor

_____
Lessee

STATE OF   }
COUNTY OF   }

On   before me,   , personally appeared , personally known to me (or proved to me on the basis of satisfactory evidence) to be the person(s) whose name(s) is/are subscribed to the within instrument and acknowledged to me that he/she/they executed the same in his/her/their authorized capacity(ies), and that by his/her/their signature(s) on the instrument the person(s), or the entity upon behalf of which the person(s) acted, executed the instrument. WITNESS my hand and official seal.

Signature_____

Affiant   _____Known   _____Unknown
ID Produced_____

(Seal)

NOTICE OF ORGANIZATION MEETING
OF INCORPORATORS AND DIRECTORS

To:

You are hereby notified that:

We, the undersigned, do hereby constitute a majority of the directors named in the Articles of Incorporation of   ,

a corporation.

Pursuant to state law, we are hereby calling an organization meeting of the Board of Directors and incorporators named in the Articles of Incorporation of the above named corporation. The purpose of said meeting is to adopt bylaws, elect officers, and transact such other business as may come before the meeting; and

Said organization meeting shall be held at

                                                on   , 19   , at

o'clock   .m.

_____   _____

_____   _____

RECEIPT OF NOTICE

_____   _____

Director   Date Received

_____

Address

NOTICE OF PRIVATE SALE
OF COLLATERAL

Date:

To:

      Pursuant to the Uniform Commercial Code you are notified that on   ,
19   , the undersigned as secured party-in-possession shall sell at private sale the following collateral:

      Said collateral shall be sold to   (Buyer), for the amount of $.

      You will be held liable for any deficiency resulting from said sale.

      You may redeem this collateral by paying the amount due plus accrued costs of foreclosure at any time prior to the time of sale. You shall have no right to redeem the property after the sale.

      The balance due as of this date (including accrued costs) is $. All payments must be by certified or bank check.

_____

Certified Mail

NOTICE OF PUBLIC SALE
OF COLLATERAL

Date:

To:

Pursuant to the Uniform Commercial Code you are provided notice that the collateral covered under our security agreement shall be sold at public auction as follows:

Date:

Time:

Location:

You will be held liable for any deficiency resulting from said sale.

You may redeem the collateral by paying the amount due and accrued costs of foreclosure at any time prior to the time of sale. You shall have no right to redeem the property after the sale.

The balance as of this date (including costs) is $. All payments must be by certified or bank check.

_____

Certified Mail

NOTICE OF PURCHASE MONEY
SECURITY INTEREST

Date:

To:

    We hereby notify you that the undersigned has or expects to acquire a purchase money security interest in and to the following described collateral:

    The said collateral shall be sold to: (Debtor)

_____

_____

_____

    Since you have an existing lien or security interest on record against the Debtor relating to the same category or collateral (pursuant to Article 9, of the Uniform Commercial Code), this notice shall inform you of our priority claim to the property being sold. The date of sale shall be on or after _____ , 19____ .

                                    Very truly,

_____

NOTICE OF RENT ARREARS

Date:

To:

     You are hereby notified that our monthly rental payment of

dollars ($) was due on or before   , and it has not been received

to date. If said sum is not paid by   , I shall invoke the remedies made

available to me under Section   of a certain lease agreement between us dated

        , relating to failure to pay the agreed rent.

_____

NOTICE OF RESCISSION

Date:

To:

Dear

     We have entered into the following described transaction with you on   ,

19   :

     A copy of our contract is enclosed.

     We hereby notify you of our rescinding of said contract, which rescission is made within

three (3) days from the contract date.

     Pursuant to the Federal Truth in Lending Act, we hereby request the return of our deposit

in the amount of $ and the cancellation of any lien against our property, and request

same within ten (10) days as required by law.

                     Very truly,

_____

CERTIFIED MAIL, Return Receipt Requested

NOTICE OF RESULTS OF PUBLIC SALE

Date:

To:

     Please take notice that on   , 19   , the public resale of goods which had been identified in a certain agreement dated   , 19   , consisting of

                             ,

was held in accordance with the notice sent to you on   , 19   .

     Said goods were resold at auction for $, which was less than our agreed price of $. Accordingly, I am holding you liable under for said amount, together with incidental expenses of $.

     If you do not remit the total amount of $ within   days, I shall refer the matter to my attorney for collection.

                    Very truly,

                    _____

NOTICE OF TERMINATION
DUE TO WORK RULES VIOLATION

DATE:

TO:

You are hereby given notice that your employment with the company shall be terminated

on   , 19 .

This action is necessary due to the following violations of company work rules:

Your final paycheck shall be for the period ending   . There shall

be no severance pay since your termination was for just cause. Please contact

concerning insurance coverage or other accrued benefits to which you may be

entitled.

We regret this action is necessary and wish you success in your future endeavors.

Sincerely,

_____

NOTICE OF UNPAID INVOICE

Date:

To:

Dear

On   , 19   , we received your check for $ representing

payment on the following invoice(s):

Invoice(s)	Amount

However, this did not include payment on the following overdue invoice(s) which remain

unpaid, and are now overdue.

Invoice(s)	Amount

In reviewing your account we assume the unpaid invoice(s) are due to oversight. Please

advise if you need copies of the unpaid invoice(s) or if there is a question regarding the

invoice(s), otherwise we shall anticipate prompt payment on these outstanding invoice(s). The

total balance due is $.

We look forward to your prompt attention to this matter.

Very truly,

_____

NOTICE OF WRONGFUL REFUSAL TO ACCEPT DELIVERY

Date:

To:

Reference is made to your order dated   , 19   , a copy of which is attached.

We have shipped said order in accordance with its terms but you have refused to accept delivery of said goods and therefore we consider the purchase contract to have been wrongfully terminated by you.

Accordingly, we shall not attempt further shipment and shall hold you liable for all damages arising from your failure to fulfill your obligations under the order.

Should you wish to rectify the situation by now accepting shipment then you must call us immediately and we shall arrange re-shipment at your expense.

Should you have any questions on this matter, then please notify us immediately.

Very truly,

_____

NOTICE TO CANCEL BACK-ORDERED GOODS

Date:

To:

Dear

    Reference is made to our purchase order dated   , 19   , a copy of which is attached.

    We have received a partial shipment and notice that certain goods on said order are out of stock or on back order.

    Please cancel our order for the back-ordered goods and adjust our invoice accordingly to reflect only the goods received. If the back-ordered goods are in transit to us, please advise us at once and we shall issue further instructions.

             Very truly,

_____

NOTICE TO CANCEL DELAYED GOODS

Date:

To:

Dear

    Reference is made to our purchase order or contract dated   , 19 ,
a copy of which is attached.

    Under the terms of said order, the goods were to be shipped by   ,
19 , or such further reasonable time as allowed by law.

    Due to your failure to ship the goods within the time required, we hereby cancel said order, reserving such further rights and remedies as we may have, including damage claims under the Uniform Commercial Code.

    If said goods are in transit, they shall be refused or returned at your expense and we shall await shipping instructions.

                     Very truly,

_____

NOTICE TO CORRECT CREDIT REPORT

Date:

To:

Dear

A review of my credit report discloses the following adverse credit information:

This information is erroneous or incomplete in the following respects:

In accordance with the provisions of the Fair Credit Reporting Act, I request that this letter be made part of my credit file and thereupon disseminated with any credit request on me. I further request that this be investigated further with the named creditor, and that unless substantiated, then said entry be deleted.

Very truly,

_____

Name

_____

Address

_____

_____

Social Security Number

NOTICE TO DIRECTORS OF SPECIAL MEETING

Date:

        A special meeting of the Board of Directors of   will be held on   , 19   , at   .m., in the offices of the Corporation located at   , in the City of   , to deliberate the following matter:

_____

Secretary

NOTICE TO EXERCISE LEASE OPTION

Date:

To:

Dear

    Reference is made to a certain lease between us dated   , 19 ,
for premises at

           .

    Under the terms of said lease we have the option to extend or renew said lease for a
term of   years commencing on   , 19 .

    This notice is provided to advise you of our intention to exercise the option to so renew
or extend the lease on the terms therein contained.

_____
                      Lessee

Certified Mail, Return Receipt

NOTICE TO LANDLORD TO MAKE REPAIRS

Date:

To:

You are hereby notified to make the following repairs:

on the premises at:

I request you to make such repairs and to do all other acts necessary to put the premises in good repair pursuant to the provisions contained in a certain lease between us dated

.

_____

NOTICE TO PAY RENT OR QUIT

TO: _____   Date:
                    Tenant

_____
                    Address

_____

    Notice to you and all others in possession of the below premises, that you are hereby notified to **vacate, quit and deliver up** the premises you hold as our tenant, namely: (Describe premises)

_____

_____

_____

    You are to deliver up said premises on or within   days of receipt of this notice, pursuant to applicable state law.

    This notice is provided due to non-payment of rent. The present rent arrearage is in the amount of $ according to the below account.

    You may reinstate your tenancy by full payment of said arrears within   days as provided under the terms of your tenancy or by applicable state law. In the event you fail to bring your rent payments current or vacate the premises, we shall immediately take legal action to evict you and to recover rents and damages for the unlawful detention of said premises together with such future rents as may be due us for breach of your tenancy agreement.

_____   _____
Owner   Address

By _____   _____
Agent   Tel. No.

PROOF OF SERVICE

    I, the undersigned, being at least eighteen years of age, declare under penalty of perjury that I served the within notice to pay rent or quit tenancy, of which this is a true copy, on the above-named tenant in the manner indicated below on   , 19   :

    ____ I personally delivered a copy of the notice to tenant.
    ____ I mailed a true copy of the notice to tenant by certified mail.
    ____ I mailed a true copy of this notice to tenant by first-class mail.

Executed on   , 19   , at

    By_____

NOTICE TO PURCHASER OF BREACH OF OPTION

Date:

To:

Please take notice that, as you have

, in violation of the provisions of a certain option, dated

, to purchase real property and by which you hold possession of

that property, the option, and all rights, title, and interest under said option is hereby terminated

and you are given   days from receipt of this notice to surrender possession to the

undersigned.

_____

NOTICE TO RECLAIM GOODS

Date:

To:

Dear

Reference is made to certain goods that have been shipped and received by you within the past ten (10) days as represented by the attached invoices.

It has come to our attention that your firm is insolvent, and therefore pursuant to the Uniform Commercial Code we demand return and reclamation of all goods delivered to you within the ten (10) days preceding this notice.

In the event any of the aforesaid goods have been sold, this shall constitute a priority claim for the value of said goods not available for return and demand is made for the return of the balance of said goods within your possession.

Please advise as to shipping arrangements.

Very truly,

_____

NOTICE TO REDIRECT PAYMENTS

Date:

To:

      You are hereby notified that effective   , 19   , the party to whom

payments should be made pursuant to our agreement dated   , 19   ,

is   , at the following address:

_____

NOTICE TO REMEDY DEFAULT BY TENANT

Date:

To:

       Take notice that you have failed to   , which you are required to do pursuant to clause   of the lease under which you occupy the premises located at: . You are further notified that if you fail to comply with said clause within   days of receipt of this notice, the undersigned will proceed to terminate this lease according to the terms of said lease.

_____

NOTICE TO SHAREHOLDERS
OF ANNUAL MEETING

Notice is hereby given that the Annual Meeting of Shareholders of

shall be held for the purpose of electing a Board of Directors for the ensuing year

and transacting such other business as may properly come before the board. The meeting, will be

held on the   day of   , 19   , at   .m., at   ,

City of   , and State of   .

Transfer books will remain closed from the   day of   , 19   , until

the   day of   , 19   .

Dated the   day of   , 19   .

By Order of the Board of Directors

_____

Secretary

NOTICE TO STOP CREDIT CHARGE

Date:

To:

Dear

    Please be advised that on   , 19   , the undersigned charged the sum of

$ on a transaction with   (Company).

    We hereby instruct you not to honor said charge or issue payment to the company for the

following reason:

    Thank you for your cooperation.

_____
Cardholder

_____
Address

_____

_____
Credit Card Number

CERTIFIED MAIL, Return Receipt Requested

NOTICE TO STOP GOODS IN TRANSIT

Date:

To:

Dear

You are in receipt of certain goods in transit shipped by us and scheduled for delivery to the following consignee:

_____

_____

_____

_____

A copy of our shipping documents is enclosed.

You are hereby instructed to stop transit of said goods, not to make delivery to the consignee and to return said goods to us. We shall pay return freight charges.

No negotiable bill of lading or document of title has been delivered to our customer (consignee).

Very truly,

_____

Copy to:

_____

Customer

NOTICE TO TENANT TO MAKE REPAIRS

Date:

To:

You are hereby notified that the repairs specified in the attached schedule, marked as Exhibit A, are required on the premises now occupied by you located at:

and I request you to make such repairs and to do all other acts necessary to put the premises in good repair pursuant to your responsibilities as contained in your lease for the said premises dated   , 19   .

                                                    _____

OFFER TO PURCHASE REAL ESTATE

BE IT KNOWN, the undersigned   of

(Buyer) offers to purchase from   of

(Owner), real estate known as   ,

City/Town of   , County of   , State of

, said property more particularly described as:

and containing   square feet of land, more or less.

The purchase price is	$
Deposit herewith paid	$
Upon signing sales agreement	$
Balance at closing	$_____
Total purchase price	$

This offer is subject to Buyer obtaining a real estate mortgage for no less than

$ payable over   years with interest not to exceed   %   at

customary terms within   days from date hereof.

The broker to this transaction is   who shall be paid a

commission of   by seller upon closing.

This offer is further subject to Buyer obtaining a satisfactory home inspection report and

termite/pest report within   days from date hereof.

Said property is to be sold free and clear of all encumbrances, by good and marketable

title, with full possession of said property available to Buyer.

The parties agree to execute a standard purchase and sales agreement according to the

terms of this agreement within   days.

The closing shall be on or before   , 19   , at the deed recording office.

Signed this   day of   , 19   .

In the presence of:

_____   _____
Witness   Broker

_____   _____
Witness   Buyer

                                                         _____
                                                         Owner

OPEN LISTING REALTY AGREEMENT

1.   This agreement signed on the   day of   , 19   , by and between

(Owner) and

(Real Estate Broker) who agree as follows:

2.   Listing term. Owner lists the property described in Paragraph 3, with the Real Estate Broker for a period of   days, from date hereof.

3.   Description of Property. The property listed is located at

4.   Commission. The Owner agrees to pay the Real Estate Broker a commission of   % of the sale price should the Broker find a purchaser ready, willing, and able to pay at least $ for the property or such other sum as may be accepted by Owner. Said commissions are payable upon closing.

5.   Non-Exclusive. The Owner retains the right to sell the property directly on his or her own behalf with no sales commission to broker, so long as the Broker did not find this purchaser. The Owner further has the right to list the property with other brokers. If a sale is made within   months after this agreement terminates to parties found by the Real Estate Agent during the term of this agreement, and wherein the buyer has been disclosed to the Owner, the Owner shall pay the commission specified above.

6.   Forfeit of Deposit. If a deposit of money is forfeited by a purchaser produced by Broker, one half shall be retained by the Broker, providing that this amount does not exceed the commission, and one half shall be paid to the Owner.

Witnessed:

_____   _____
Witness   Owner

_____   _____
Witness   Broker

OPTION TO PURCHASE

OPTION AGREEMENT by and between

(Owner) and   (Buyer).

1.   Buyer hereby pays to Owner the sum of $ in consideration for this option, which option payment shall be credited to the purchase price if the option is exercised.

2.   Buyer has the option and right to buy

(property) within the option period for the full price of $.

3.   This option shall remain in effect until   , 19   , and thereupon expire unless this option is sooner exercised.

4.   To exercise this option, Buyer must notify Owner of same by certified mail within the option period. All notices shall be sent to owner at the following address:

_____

_____

_____

5.   Should the Buyer exercise the option, the Owner and Buyer agree to promptly sign the attached contract of sale, and consummate the sale on its terms, which are incorporated herein by reference.

6.   This option agreement shall be binding upon and inure to the benefit of the parties, their successors, assigns and personal representatives.

Signed this   day of   , 19   .

_____   _____

Owner   Buyer

OPTION TO PURCHASE STOCK

      In consideration of   dollars ($),

the receipt of which is hereby acknowledged, the undersigned,   ,

hereby gives to   for a period of

days from the date hereof, the right to purchase   shares of the   stock of

                         at the price of   dollars ($)

per share. This option can be exercised only by the payment of cash before its expiration.

Date:

_____

ORGAN DONATION
of

_____

In the hope that I may help others, I hereby make this anatomical gift, if medically acceptable, for the purposes of transplantation, to take effect upon my death.

The words and marks below indicate my desires:

I give: a)_____any needed organs.

b)_____only the following organs for purposes of

transplantation, therapy, education or medical research:

c)_____my entire body, for anatomical or medical study, if needed.

Limitations or special wishes:

Signed by the donor and following two witnesses, in the presence of each other.

_____   _____

Signature of Donor   Birth date

_____   _____

Date Signed   City and State

_____   _____

Witness   Witness

PARTIAL RELEASE OF LIEN

KNOW ALL MEN BY THESE PRESENTS:

That the undersigned, for and in consideration of the payment of the sum of
                                    Dollars ($) paid by   ,
receipt of which is hereby acknowledged, hereby releases
          dollars ($) from the amount due under its lien against the following described premises:

on account of labor performed and/or materials furnished for the improvement of the above described premises. This partial release does not release the lien or the lien rights which undersigned has or may acquire because of labor performed or materials furnished for the improvement of the above described premises and any such lien or lien rights shall relate to and take effect from the date of recording the NOTICE OF COMMENCEMENT or NOTICE TO OWNER provided under applicable state law.

         IN WITNESS WHEREOF, I have hereunto set my hand and seal this   day of
                    , 19   .

Signed in the presence of:

_____   _____
Witness   Lienholder

                                                                 _____
                                                                 Lienholder

STATE OF
COUNTY OF   }
On   before me,   , personally appeared
                                                        , personally known to me (or
proved to me on the basis of satisfactory evidence) to be the person(s) whose name(s) is/are subscribed to the within instrument and acknowledged to me that he/she/they executed the same in his/her/their authorized capacity(ies), and that by his/her/their signature(s) on the instrument the person(s), or the entity upon behalf of which the person(s) acted, executed the instrument.
WITNESS my hand and official seal.
Signature_____

                                        Affiant   _____Known   _____Unknown
                                        ID Produced_____
                                                                                (Seal)

PARTIAL SHIPMENT REQUEST

Date:

To:

Dear

     Thank you for your order dated   , 19 . The amount of the order is approximately $, however, we regret we cannot extend you credit for the entire amount at the present time.

     Accordingly we suggest we ship you on our standard credit terms a partial order reducing quantities by   percent. Upon payment we shall release the balance of the order. If you request a different order configuration we would, of course, be pleased to accommodate you.

     Unless we hear from you to the contrary within the next ten (10) days, we shall assume you accept our recommendation and we shall ship accordingly.

     Hopefully, we shall soon be in a position to increase your credit line.

Very truly,

_____

PARTNERSHIP ACKNOWLEDGEMENT

STATE OF

COUNTY OF

}

On the   day of   , 19   , before me personally appeared,

, known to me, or proved to me on the basis of satisfactory

evidence to be one of the partners that executed the within instrument, and thereupon

acknowledged to me that said partnership executed the same.

On   before me,   , personally appeared
, personally known to me (or
proved to me on the basis of satisfactory evidence) to be the person(s) whose name(s) is/are
subscribed to the within instrument and acknowledged to me that he/she/they executed the same
in his/her/their authorized capacity(ies), and that by his/her/their signature(s) on the instrument
the person(s), or the entity upon behalf of which the person(s) acted, executed the instrument.
WITNESS my hand and official seal.

Signature_____

Affiant   _____Known   _____Unknown
ID Produced_____
(Seal)

PARTNERSHIP AGREEMENT

AGREEMENT by and between the Undersigned

("Partners").

1.   Name. The name of the partnership is:

2.   Partners. The names of the initial partners are:

3.   Place of Business. The principal place of business of the partnership is:

4.   Nature of Business. The partnership shall generally engage in the following business:

5.   Duration. The partnership shall commence business on   and shall continue until terminated by this agreement, or by operation of law.

6.   Contribution of Capital. The partners shall contribute capital in proportionate shares as follows:

Partner	Capital	Partnership Shares
_____	_____	_____
_____	_____	_____
_____	_____	_____
_____	_____	_____

7.   Allocation of Depreciation or Gain or Loss on Contributed Property. The partners understand that, for income tax purposes, the partnership's adjusted basis of some of the contributed property differs from fair market value at which the property was accepted by the partnership. However, the partners intend that the general allocation rule of the Internal Revenue Code shall apply, and that the depreciation or gain or loss arising with respect to this property shall be allocated proportionately between the partners, as allocated in Paragraph 6 above, in determining the taxable income or loss of the partnership and the distributive share of each partner, in the same manner as if such property had been purchased by the partnership at a cost equal to the adjusted tax basis.

8.   Capital Accounts. An individual capital account shall be maintained for each partner. The capital of each partner shall consist of that partner's original contribution of capital, as described in Paragraph 6, and increased by additional capital contributions and decreased by distributions in reduction of partnership capital and reduced by his/her share of partnership losses, if these losses are charged to the capital accounts.

9.   Drawing Accounts. An individual drawing account shall be maintained for each partner. All withdrawals by a partner shall be charged to his drawing account. Withdrawals shall be limited to amounts unanimously agreed to by the partners.

10.   Salaries. No partner shall receive any salary for services rendered to the partnership except as specifically and first approved by each of the partners.

11.   Loans by Partners. If a majority of partners consent, any partner may lend money to the partnership at an interest and terms rate agreed in writing, at the time said loan is made.

12.   Profits and Losses. Net profits of the partnership shall be divided proportionately between the partners, and the net losses shall be borne proportionately as follows:

Partner   Proportion

_____   _____

_____   _____

_____   _____

13.   Management. The partners shall have equal rights and control in the management of the partnership.

14.   Books of Accounts. The partnership shall maintain adequate accounting records. All books, records, and accounts of the partnership shall be open at all times to inspection by all partners, or their designated representatives.

15.   Accounting Basis. The books of account shall be kept on a cash basis.

16.   Fiscal Year. The books of account shall be kept on a fiscal year basis, commencing January 1 and ending December 31, and shall be closed and balanced at the end of each year.

17.   Annual Audit. The books of account shall be audited as of the close of each fiscal year by an accountant chosen by the partners.

18.   Banking. All funds of the partnership shall be deposited in the name of the partnership into such checking or savings accounts as designated by the partners.

19.   Death or Incapacity. The death or incapacity of a partner shall cause an immediate dissolution of the partnership.

20.   Election of Remaining Partner to Continue Business. In the event of the retirement, death, incapacity, or insanity of a partner, the remaining partners shall have the right to continue the business of the partnership, either by themselves or in conjunction with any other person or persons they may select, but they shall pay to the retiring partner, or to the legal representatives of the deceased or incapacitated partner, the value of his or her interest in the partnership.

21.   Valuation of Partner's Interest. The value of the interest of a retiring, incapacitated, deceased, or insane partner shall be the sum of (a) the partner's capital account, (b) any unpaid loans due the partner, and (c) the partner's proportionate share of the accrued net profits remaining undistributed in his drawing account. No value for goodwill shall be included in determining the value of a partner's interest, unless specifically agreed in advance by the partners.

22.   Payment of Purchase Price. The value of the partner's interest shall be paid without interest to the retiring partner, or to the legal representative of the deceased, incapacitated or insane partner, in   (   ) monthly installments, commencing on the first day of the second month after the effective date of the purchase.

23.   Termination. In the event that the remaining partner does not elect to purchase the interest of the retiring, deceased, incapacitated, or insane partner, or in the event the partners mutually agree to dissolve, the partnership shall terminate and the partners shall proceed with reasonable promptness to liquidate the business of the partnership. The assets of the partnership shall first be used to pay or provide for all debts of the partnership. Thereafter, all money remaining undistributed in the drawing accounts shall be paid to the partners. Then the remaining assets shall be divided proportionately as follows:

Partner   Percentage

_____   _____

_____   _____

_____   _____

24.   This agreement shall be binding upon and inure to the benefit of the parties, their successors, assigns and personal representatives.

Signed this   day of   , 19   .

_____   _____
Witness   Partner

_____   _____
Witness   Partner

_____   _____
Witness   Partner

PAST DUE REMINDER

Date:

To:

Dear

      Please take note that your account is past due in the amount of

Dollars ($). We sent you a statement a short time ago.

      Please remit payment to us as soon as possible.

                    Thank you,

_____

PAYMENT INQUIRY

Date:

To:

Dear

     We are at a loss to understand why your account balance of $ has not been paid.

     Perhaps you can now take a moment and help resolve it. Just take a moment and let us know where we stand.

    _____ The account has not been paid because:

    _____ The account will be paid on or before   , 19   .

    _____ Our check is enclosed. Sorry for the delay.

Your above response is greatly appreciated.

                 Very truly,

_____

PAYMENT ON SPECIFIC ACCOUNTS

Date:

To:

Dear

      We enclose our Check No. _____ in the amount of $ _____ . This check is to be credited to the following charges or invoices only:

Invoice/Debt	Amount
_____	$_____
_____	$_____
_____	$_____
_____	$_____
_____	$_____

      You understand that payment herein shall be applied only to the specific items listed and shall not be applied, in whole or in part, to any other obligation, charge or invoice that may be outstanding.

      Very truly,

_____

PAYMENT ON WRITTEN INSTRUMENT

Date:

Received this day from   the sum of

dollars ($) on account of the payments

referred to in the note given by the above to me and dated   , 19   .

_____

PAYROLL DEDUCTION AUTHORIZATION

The undersigned hereby authorizes _____ to deduct

$_____ from my gross earnings each payroll period beginning _____

itemized as follows:

In payment for: Amount

____ Credit Union $_____.__

____ Employee Savings Plan   _____.__

____ 401 K Plan   _____.__

____ Union Dues   _____.__

____ _____   _____.__

____ _____   _____.__

____ _____   _____.__

____ _____   _____.__

         Total $_____.__

Signature_____ Date_____

Print Name_____

Social Security No._____

Please keep a copy of this for your records.

PERMISSION TO USE COPYRIGHTED MATERIAL

FOR GOOD CONSIDERATION, and in consideration of the sum of $
to be paid herewith, the undersigned, as copyright holder, hereby grants permission to
to reprint, publish and use for world distribution the following material:

This material shall be used only in the following manner or publication:

A credit line to acknowledge use of the material is/is not required. If required, the credit
line shall read as follows:

This agreement shall be binding upon and inure to the benefit of the parties, their
successors, assigns and personal representatives.

Signed this   day of   , 19   .

In the presence of:

_____   _____
Witness   Name

PERMISSION TO USE QUOTE OR PERSONAL STATEMENT

FOR GOOD CONSIDERATION, the undersigned irrevocably authorizes

and its successors and assigns the worldwide rights to use, publish or reprint in whole or in part, the following statement, picture, endorsement, quotation or other material:

This authorization shall extend only to a certain publication known as

, including all new editions, reprints, excerpts, advertisement, publicity and promotions thereto of said work, and further including such publications as hold subsidiary rights thereto.

The Undersigned acknowledges that the permission granted herein is non-revocable, and that no further payment is due therein.

This agreement shall be binding upon and inure to the benefit of the parties, their successors, assigns and personal representatives.

Signed this   day of   , 19   .

Witnessed:

_____   _____
Witness   Name

_____   _____
Witness   Address

                                      _____
                                      City   State   Zip

PERSONAL PROPERTY RENTAL AGREEMENT

AGREEMENT made between   (Owner) and

                              (Renter):

1.   Owner hereby rents to renter the below described personal property:

2.   Renter shall pay to Owner the sum of $ as payment for the rental herein, said sum payable as follows:

3.   The Renter shall during the rental term keep and maintain the property in good condition and repair and shall be responsible for any loss, casualty, damage or destruction to said property notwithstanding how caused and Renter agrees to return said property in its present condition, reasonable wear and tear excepted.

4.   The Renter shall not during the rental period allow others the use of the property.

5.   The rental period shall commence on   , 19   , and terminate on   , 19   , at which date the property shall be promptly returned.

6.   Other terms:

Signed this   day of   , 19   .

In the presence of:

_____   _____
Witness   Owner

                                                             _____
                                                             Renter

PLEDGE OF PERSONAL PROPERTY

BE IT KNOWN, for value received, the undersigned

(Pledgor) of   , hereby deposits, delivers to and pledges with

(Pledgee) of   , as collateral security

to secure the payment of the following described debt owing Pledgee:

The collateral consisting of the following personal property:

It is further agreed that:

1.   Pledgee may assign or transfer said debt and the pledged collateral hereunder to any third party.

2.   Pledgee shall have no liability for loss, destruction or casualty to the collateral unless caused by its own negligence, or the negligence of any assignee.

3.   The Pledgor shall pay any and all insurance it elects to maintain, or the Pledgee reasonably requires on the pledged collateral and shall pay any personal property, excise or other tax or levy.

4.   The Pledgor warrants that it has good title to the pledged collateral, full authority to pledge same and that said collateral is free of any adverse lien, encumbrance or adverse claim.

5.   Upon default of payment of the debt or breach of this pledge agreement, the Pledgee or holder shall have full rights to foreclose on the pledged collateral and exercise its rights as a secured party pursuant to Article 9 of the Uniform Commercial Code; said rights being cumulative with any other rights the Pledgee or holder may have against the Pledgor.

The Pledgor understands that upon foreclosure the pledged property may be sold at public auction or private sale. The Pledgor shall be provided reasonable notice of any said intended sale and the Pledgor shall have full rights to redeem said collateral at any time prior to said sale upon payment of the balance due hereunder together with accrued fees and expenses of collection. In the event the collateral shall be sold for less than the amount then owing, the Pledgor shall be liable for any deficiency.

Upon payment of the obligation for which the property is pledged, the property shall be returned to the Pledgor and this pledge agreement shall be terminated.

This pledge agreement shall be binding upon and inure to the benefit of the parties, their successors, assigns and personal representatives.

Upon default the Pledgor shall pay all reasonable attorneys' fees and cost of collection.

Signed this   day of   , 19   .

In the presence of:

_____   _____
Witness   Pledgor

_____   _____
Witness   Pledgee

PLEDGE OF SHARES OF STOCK

BE IT KNOWN, for value received, the undersigned
(Pledgor) of   hereby deposits, delivers to and pledges
with   (Pledgee) of
as collateral security to secure the payment of the following described debt owing Pledgee:

The shares of stock, described as   shares of stock of
(Corporation) represented as Stock Certificate No(s).

It is further agreed that:

1.   Pledgee may assign or transfer said debt and the collateral pledged hereunder to any third party.

2.   In the event a stock dividend or further issue of stock in the Corporation is issued to the Pledgor, the Pledgor shall pledge said shares as additional collateral for the debt.

3.   That during the term of this pledge agreement, and so long as it is not in default, the Pledgor shall have full rights to vote said shares and be entitled to all dividend income, except that stock dividends shall also be pledged.

4.   That during the pendency of this agreement, the Pledgor shall not issue any proxy or assignment of rights to the pledged shares.

5.   The Pledgor warrants and represents it has good title to the shares being pledged, they are free from liens and encumbrances or prior pledge, and the Pledgor has full authority to transfer said shares as collateral security.

6.   Upon default of payment of the debt, or breach of this pledge agreement, the Pledgee or holder shall have full rights to foreclose on the pledged shares and exercise its rights as a secured party pursuant to Article 9 of the Uniform Commercial Code; said rights being cumulative with any other rights the Pledgee or holder may have against the Pledgor.

The Pledgor understands that upon foreclosure the pledged shares may be sold at public auction or private sale. The Pledgor shall be provided reasonable notice of any said intended sale and the Pledgor shall have full rights to redeem said shares at any time prior to said sale upon payment of the balance due hereunder, and accrued costs of collection. In the event the shares shall be sold for less than the amount then owing, the Pledgor shall be liable for any deficiency.

Upon payment of the obligation for which the shares are pledged, the shares shall be returned to the Pledgor and this pledge agreement shall be terminated.

This pledge agreement shall be binding upon and inure to the benefit of the parties, their successors, assigns and personal representatives.

Upon default the Pledgor shall pay all reasonable attorneys' fees and cost of collection.

Signed this   day of   , 19   .

_____   _____
Witness   Pledgor

_____   _____
Witness   Pledgee

POLYGRAPH CONSENT

Name:

Date of Polygraph Examination:

I voluntarily agree to a polygraph examination on the above date.

A company representative has advised me of the following:

1)   I am guaranteed by law the right not to take this examination as a condition of employment or continued employment.

2)   I have not been coerced in any way into either taking this test or signing this consent agreement. This act is entirely voluntary on my part.

3)   I have retained a copy of this agreement for my records.

Signature_____ Date_____

POSTNUPTIAL PROPERTY AGREEMENT

This agreement made by and between   (Husband)

and   (Wife) who have been married since   , 19   , and

who reside at   ,

County of   , State of   .

This agreement is entered into with the intent and desire to specify and define the respective rights of the parties in and to the separate, joint and community property of the parties but with the express understanding that neither party wishes to obtain a divorce or legal separation.

Now, therefore, it is hereby stipulated by the parties that:

1. The Husband shall have sole and exclusive rights to the described personal and real property listed on Exhibit A, notwithstanding whether said property is presently held by Husband and Wife, jointly or as community property or other co-tenancy.

2. The Wife shall have sole and exclusive rights to the described personal and real property listed on Exhibit B, notwithstanding whether said property is presently held by Wife and Husband, jointly or as community property or other co-tenancy.

3. All property stipulated to be property of one or the other parties shall be taken subject to all present or future liens, mortgages, encumbrances or claims of record.

4. The parties shall from time to time stipulate the respective rights to marital property acquired from and after the date of this agreement.

5. All exhibits are herein incorporated by reference.

6. The parties agree to execute all documents necessary to perfect good title to the respective properties to the named spouse.

7. Both parties acknowledge that they have either been represented by separate counsel or had full opportunity to be so represented.

8. This agreement shall be binding upon and inure to the benefit of the parties, their successors, assigns and personal representatives.

Signed under seal this   day of   , 19   .

_____   _____
Husband   Wife

STATE OF   }
COUNTY OF   }

On   before me,   , personally appeared
                    , personally known to me (or
proved to me on the basis of satisfactory evidence) to be the person(s) whose name(s) is/are
subscribed to the within instrument and acknowledged to me that he/she/they executed the same
in his/her/their authorized capacity(ies), and that by his/her/their signature(s) on the instrument
the person(s), or the entity upon behalf of which the person(s) acted, executed the instrument.
WITNESS my hand and official seal.

Signature_____

                                         Affiant   _____Known   _____Unknown
                                         ID Produced_____
                                                                          (Seal)

POWER OF ATTORNEY
DELEGATING PARENTAL AUTHORITY
(With Consent for Medical Care)

BE IT KNOWN, that _____, of _____,
the undersigned parent or lawful guardian (Grantor) of _____, a minor child
(Child), does hereby grant to _____, as Custodian of said Child,
the following powers, authorities and consents:

1.   Grantor consents to the temporary custody of said Child by the Custodian for the period and purpose as follows:

2.   Grantor authorized the Custodian to do and undertake all acts as are reasonable and necessary to protect the best interests and welfare of the Child while under the care of the Custodian. Without limiting the generality of the foregoing, the Custodian is further authorized to provide emergency and general medical care which the Custodian in his or her discretion deems necessary or advisable for any illness or injury sustained by the Child during this temporary custody.

3.   Grantor consents to any reasonable discipline imposed upon Child by the Guardian provided that said discipline does not constitute unreasonable abuse.

4.   Grantor agrees to exonerate and hold harmless the Custodian and its lawful agents and employees from any loss or liability arising during this custody, excepting for any acts of ordinary negligence, gross negligence or wanton, willful or reckless conduct. Grantor specifically agrees to reimburse Custodian for any reasonable expenditures required for the proper care of said Child.

Other:

Signed this   day of   , 19   .

In the presence of:

_____   _____
Witness   Grantor

_____   _____
Witness   Custodian

STATE OF   }
COUNTY OF   }

On   before me,   , personally appeared
                                                        , personally known to me (or
proved to me on the basis of satisfactory evidence) to be the person(s) whose name(s) is/are
subscribed to the within instrument and acknowledged to me that he/she/they executed the same
in his/her/their authorized capacity(ies), and that by his/her/their signature(s) on the instrument
the person(s), or the entity upon behalf of which the person(s) acted, executed the instrument.
WITNESS my hand and official seal.

Signature_____

                                    Affiant   _____Known   _____Unknown
                                    ID Produced_____
                                                                        (Seal)

POWER OF ATTORNEY REVOCATION

Reference is made to certain power of attorney granted by

(Grantor) to   (Attorney-in-Fact), and dated

19   .

This document acknowledges and constitutes notice that the Grantor hereby revokes, rescinds and terminates said power-of-attorney and all authority, rights and power thereto effective this date.

Signed under seal this   day of   , 19   .

_____
Grantor

Acknowledged by Attorney-in-Fact:

_____

STATE OF   }
COUNTY OF

On   before me,   , personally appeared
                                    , personally known to me (or proved to me on the basis of satisfactory evidence) to be the person(s) whose name(s) is/are subscribed to the within instrument and acknowledged to me that he/she/they executed the same in his/her/their authorized capacity(ies), and that by his/her/their signature(s) on the instrument the person(s), or the entity upon behalf of which the person(s) acted, executed the instrument. WITNESS my hand and official seal.

Signature_____

                              Affiant _____Known _____Unknown
                              ID Produced_____
                                                      (Seal)

PREMARITAL AGREEMENT

BE IT KNOWN, this agreement is entered into on the   day of   , 19   ,

between   and   .

Whereas, the parties contemplate legal marriage under the laws of the State of

, and it is their mutual desire to enter into this agreement so that

they will continue to own and control their own property, and are getting married because of

their love for each other but do not desire that their present respective financial interests be

changed by their marriage. Now, therefore, it is agreed as follows:

1. All property which belongs to each of the above parties shall be, and shall forever
   remain, their personal estate, including all interest, rents, and profits which may
   accrue from said property, and said property shall remain forever free of claim by
   the other.

2. The parties shall have at all times the full right and authority, in all respects the
   same as each would have it not married, to use, sell, enjoy, manage, gift and
   convey all property as may presently belong to him or her.

3. In the event of a separation or divorce, the parties shall have no right against each
   other by way of claims for support, alimony, maintenance, compensation or
   division of property existing of this date.

4. In the event of separation or divorce, marital property acquired after marriage
   shall nevertheless remain subject to division, either by agreement or judicial
   determination.

5. This agreement shall be binding upon and inure to the benefit of the parties, their
   successors, assigns and personal representatives.

This agreement shall be enforced with the laws of the State of   .

Signed this   day of   , 19   .

Witnessed:

_____

Witness   First Party

_____

Witness   Second Party

PRESENTMENT BY MAIL

Date:

To:

      The undersigned,   of   ,

is the holder of a certain instrument, dated   , made by you for the

payment of   dollars ($)

on   , 19   , to the order of   of

           . The undersigned, being the present

holder of said instrument, hereby demands payment of this note.

                                     _____

PRIVACY RELEASE

Agreement made this   day of   , 19   , that in consideration of

                    Dollars ($), receipt of which is acknowledged, I,

                    , do hereby grant   and his or her

assigns, licensees, and legal representatives the irrevocable right to use my name (or any

fictional name), picture, portrait, or photograph in all forms and media in all manners, including

composite or distorted representations, for advertising, trade, or any other lawful purposes, and I

waive any right to inspect or approve the finished version(s), including written copy that may be

created in connection therewith. I am of lawful age.* I have read this release and am fully

familiar with its contents.

_____   _____
Witness   Grantor

_____   _____
Address   Address

Consent (if applicable)

I am the parent or guardian of the minor named above and have the legal authority to

execute the above release I approve the foregoing and consent to same on behalf of said minor.

_____   _____
Witness   Parent or Guardian

_____   _____
Address   Address

Date:

* Delete this sentence if the subject is a minor. The parent or guardian must then sign the consent.

PRODUCT DEFECT CLAIM

Date:

To:

Dear

We have sold to a customer a product sold or manufactured by you named and described as:

We have been advised by the customer of a product defect or warranty claim in the following particulars:

Name of Customer:

Date of Purchase:

Claimed Defect:

Injuries or Damage Claimed:

In the event suit or claim is brought against us arising from breach of warranty of merchantability, or any such similar claim arising from said product, we shall in a like manner look to you for full reimbursement and indemnification.

This letter is provided to give you earliest possible notice of a potential claim, and to preserve our rights against you should such a claim arise.

We shall advise you upon receipt of any further information on this claim.

Very truly,

_____

PRODUCT DEFECT NOTICE

Date:

To:

Dear

    Notice is hereby provided that we have purchased a product manufactured, distributed or sold by you and described as:

    You are advised of a product defect or warranty claim. In support of same we provide the following information:

1. <u>Date of Purchase</u>:

2. <u>Nature of Defect</u>:

3. <u>Injuries or Damage</u>:

4. <u>Item Purchased From</u>:

    This is provided to give you earliest possible notice of said claim. I request that you or your representative contact me as soon as possible.

Very truly,

_____

Name

_____

Address

_____

City, State, Zip

_____

Telephone Number

CERTIFIED MAIL, Return Receipt Requested

PRODUCT WARRANTY CLAIM

Date:

To:

Dear

Please be advised that we purchased the following named product,

from   , on   , 19   .

This product is defective or in need of repair in the following particulars:

This product is under a full warranty and we therefore request repair of the product under

the warranty terms.

Accordingly:

_____ Product is enclosed for repair/replacement and return.

_____ Please call (   ) for a service appointment.

Thank you for your cooperation in this matter.

Very truly,

_____

Name

_____

Address

_____

City, State, Zip

_____

Telephone

PROMISSORY NOTE

Principal amount $ Date:

FOR VALUE RECEIVED, the undersigned hereby jointly and severally promise to pay to the order of   the sum of

Dollars ($), together with interest thereon at the rate of   % per annum on the unpaid balance. Said sum shall be paid in the manner following:

All payments shall be first applied to interest and the balance to principal. This note may be prepaid, at any time, in whole or in part, without penalty.

This note shall at the option of any holder thereof be immediately due and payable upon the occurrence of any of the following: 1) Failure to make any payment due hereunder within days of its due date. 2) Breach of any condition of any security interest, mortgage, loan agreement, pledge agreement or guarantee granted as collateral security for this note. 3) Breach of any condition of any loan agreement, security agreement or mortgage, if any, having a priority over any loan agreement, security agreement or mortgage on collateral granted, in whole or in part, as collateral security for this note. 4) Upon the death, incapacity, dissolution or liquidation of any of the undersigned, or any endorser, guarantor to surety hereto. 5) Upon the filing by any of the undersigned of an assignment for the benefit of creditors, bankruptcy or other form of insolvency, or by suffering an involuntary petition in bankruptcy or receivership not vacated within thirty (30) days.

In the event this note shall be in default and placed for collection, then the undersigned agree to pay all reasonable attorney fees and costs of collection. Payments not made within five (5) days of due date shall be subject to a late charge of   % of said payment. All payments hereunder shall be made to such address as may from time to time be designated by any holder.

The undersigned and all other parties to this note, whether as endorsers, guarantors or sureties, agree to remain fully bound until this note shall be fully paid and waive demand, presentment and protest and all notices hereto and further agree to remain bound, notwithstanding any extension, modification, waiver, or other indulgence or discharge or release of any obligor hereunder or exchange, substitution, or release of any collateral granted as security for this note. No modification or indulgence by any holder hereof shall be binding unless in writing; and any indulgence on any one occasion shall not be an indulgence for any other or future occasion. Any modification or change in terms, hereunder granted by any holder hereof, shall be valid and binding upon each of the undersigned, notwithstanding the acknowledgement of any of the undersigned, and each of the undersigned does hereby irrevocably grant to each of the others a power of attorney to enter into any such modification on their behalf. The rights of any holder hereof shall be cumulative and not necessarily successive. This note shall take effect as a sealed instrument and shall be construed, governed and enforced in accordance with the laws of the State of   .

Witnessed:

_____   _____
Witness   Borrower

_____   _____
Witness   Borrower

GUARANTY

We the undersigned jointly and severally guaranty the prompt and punctual payment of all moneys due under the aforesaid note and agree to remain bound until fully paid.

In the presence of:

_____   _____
Witness   Guarantor

_____   _____
Witness   Guarantor

PROPOSAL TO BUY A BUSINESS

Date:

To:

Re: Purchase of

The undersigned is interested in negotiating an agreement for the purchase and sale as a going concern of all the business assets, including furniture, fixtures and equipment, stock in trade, parts and supplies, leasehold interest and goodwill, owned by you in connection with the business carried on as

located at   .

Subject to formal contract, we are prepared to pay $ for the business on the following terms:

If you are interested in selling at this price on these terms, please let us know and we will make you a formal offer to purchase.

Very truly,

_____

PROXY TO VOTE CORPORATE SHARES

BE IT KNOWN, that the undersigned,   of
being the owner of   shares of voting common stock of
(Corporation) does hereby grant to   a proxy and appoint
him my attorney-in-fact to vote on behalf of the undersigned   shares of said stock at any
future general or special meeting of the stockholders of the Corporation, and said proxyholder is
entitled to attend said meetings and act on my behalf and vote said share personally or through
mail proxy, all to the same extent as if I voted said shares personally.

During the pendency of this proxy, all rights to vote said shares shall be held by the
proxyholder with full power of substitution or revocation, provided the undersigned may revoke
this proxy at any time, upon written notice of termination by certified mail, return receipt, to
both the proxyholder and to the corporation.

The proxyholder shall be entitled to reimbursement for reasonable expenses incurred
hereunder, but otherwise shall not be entitled to compensation for the services to be rendered.

This agreement shall be binding upon and inure to the benefit of the parties, their
successors, assigns and personal representatives.

IN WITNESS WHEREOF, I have executed this proxy this   day of   , 19 .
Accepted:

_____   _____
Proxyholder   Stockholder

STATE OF   }
COUNTY OF   }

On   before me,   , personally appeared
                                        , personally known to me (or
proved to me on the basis of satisfactory evidence) to be the person(s) whose name(s) is/are
subscribed to the within instrument and acknowledged to me that he/she/they executed the same
in his/her/their authorized capacity(ies), and that by his/her/their signature(s) on the instrument
the person(s), or the entity upon behalf of which the person(s) acted, executed the instrument.
WITNESS my hand and official seal.

Signature_____

                         Affiant   _____Known   _____Unknown
                         ID Produced_____
                                                    (Seal)

PURCHASE REQUIREMENT AGREEMENT

FOR GOOD CONSIDERATION, the undersigned hereby agrees to enter into this purchase requirement on the following terms:

1. During the period from   , 19   , to   , 19   , the undersigned shall purchase from supplier, goods in the following quantity: (Describe amount/time period or % of purchase requirements.)

2. The undersigned shall pay for said purchases within the supplier's credit terms, or such extended terms as shall be expressly approved in writing by Supplier.

3. All purchases hereunder shall further be at such prices and include all promotional or advertising allowances, cash and/or trade discounts and other incentives and inducements, if any, as then customarily available to other accounts purchasing from Supplier on equally proportioned terms.

4. In the event the undersigned shall fail to meet the above described purchase requirements, or otherwise default under this agreement, then in such event, Supplier shall have full rights to demand immediate payment of all sums due Supplier notwithstanding extended terms evidenced by any note, extension agreement or other agreement authorizing extended terms.

    Signed this   day of   , 19   .

_____   _____
Customer   Supplier

PURCHASER'S ASSIGNMENT OF OPTION

In consideration of   Dollars ($) paid to the undersigned, receipt of which is hereby acknowledged, the undersigned hereby sells, assigns, and transfers, to

all my right, title, and interest as purchaser in the option to purchase property dated   , executed by   as seller to me as purchaser, covering certain property described as:

The undersigned represents to the assignee that the option has not been exercised, that the period thereof will expire on   , and that the option has not been rescinded or modified.

Signed this   day of   , 19   .

In the presence of:

_____   _____
Witness   Purchaser

QUITCLAIM BILL OF SALE

BE IT KNOWN, for good consideration, and in consideration of the payment of $, the receipt and sufficiency of which is acknowledged, the undersigned (Seller) hereby sells, transfers, assigns and conveys unto and its successors and assigns forever with quitclaim covenants only, the following described property:

Seller hereby sells and transfers only such right, title and interest as it may hold and that said chattels sold herein are sold subject to such prior liens, encumbrances and adverse claims, if any, that may exist, and Seller disclaims any and all warranties thereto.

Said assets are further sold in "as is" condition and where presently located.

Signed this   day of   , 19   .

In the presence of:

_____   _____
Witness   Seller

QUITCLAIM DEED

THIS QUITCLAIM DEED, Executed this _____ day of _____, 19 _____ ,

by first party, _____

whose post office address is _____

to second party, _____

whose post office address is _____

WITNESSETH, That the said first party, for good consideration and for the sum of _____ Dollars ($ _____) paid by the said second party, the receipt whereof is hereby acknowledged, does hereby remise, release and quitclaim unto the said second party forever, all the right, title, interest and claim which the said first party has in and to the following described parcel of land, and improvements and appurtenances thereto in the County of _____, State of _____ to wit:

IN WITNESS WHEREOF, The said first party has signed and sealed these presents the day and year first above written. Signed, sealed and delivered in presence of:

_____
Signature of Witness

_____
Print name of Witness

_____
Signature of Witness

_____
Print name of Witness

_____
Signature of First Party

_____
Print name of First Party

_____
Signature of First Party

_____
Print name of First Party

State of _____ }
County of _____
On _____ before me, _____ ,
appeared _____
personally known to me (or proved to me on the basis of satisfactory evidence) to be the person(s) whose name(s) is/are subscribed to the within instrument and acknowledged to me that he/she/they executed the same in his/her/their authorized capacity(ies), and that by his/her/their signature(s) on the instrument the person(s), or the entity upon behalf of which the person(s) acted, executed the instrument.
WITNESS my hand and official seal.

_____
Signature of Notary

Affiant _____ Known _____ Produced ID
Type of ID _____
(Seal)

RECEIPT

BE IT KNOWN, that the undersigned hereby acknowledges receipt of the sum of

$ paid by   which payment constitutes

payment of the below described obligation:

If this is in partial payment of said obligation the remaining unpaid balance on this date

is $.

Signed this   day of   , 19   .

Witnessed:

_____   _____

RECEIPT FOR BALANCE OF ACCOUNT

Date:

      Received from   the sum of

dollars ($), being the balance of account due to the undersigned as of this date.

_____

RECEIPT IN FULL—ALL DEMANDS

Date:

      Received from   , the sum of

Dollars

($), in full payment of all demands.

_____

RECEIPT IN FULL BY AN AGENT

Date:

Received from   the sum of

Dollars ($) in full discharge of all claims which the undersigned has as of this date.

_____

By:_____, Agent

RECEIPT IN FULL BY AN AGENT TO AN AGENT

Date:

Received from _____, agent for _____, the sum of _____ dollars ($) in full discharge of all claims which _____ has against him or her up to date.

_____

By:_____, Agent

RECEIPT OF NOTE FOR COLLECTION

Date:

       The undersigned received from   , for collection, a note, dated   , 19   , signed by   and payable to   , for

dollars ($) with interest from   , at the rate of

percent (%), which note the undersigned is to use best endeavors to collect, and to put the

same in judgment at the costs of $ if not paid on presentation; to retain   percent

(%) of the amount actually collected for my services, and to pay the remainder to   , but in no wise to become responsible for costs, or

to guarantee the collection of the same.

_____

RECEIPT ON ACCOUNT FOR GOODS TO BE DELIVERED

Date:

     Received from   the sum of

dollars ($) on account of the price of the purchase of:

to be delivered on or before   , 19   .

_____

RECEIPT ON ACCOUNT FOR PARTIAL PAYMENT

Date:

Received from _____, the sum of

dollars ($ _____), on account, as partial payment of the principal amount of $ _____ .

_____

REFERRAL OF CLAIM FOR COLLECTION

Name of Collection Agency:
Address:
Telephone:

Creditor:
Address:
Telephone:

     The account described herein is referred to you for collection.

     Unless we advise you of payment within   days, you may proceed with whatever steps are necessary for collection of this account, subject to the restriction set forth.

     Payments collected by you or paid directly to us after the expiration of said period are subject to a collection commission as set forth in your commission schedule.

     You are hereby authorized to endorse in our name for deposit and collection all payments received on this account.

     It is understood that you are not authorized to initiate legal proceedings with respect to the described account.

     If you are unable to collect the amount owed in the account you may return it to us for submission to our attorneys.

DESCRIPTION OF ACCOUNT

Debtor: _____

Address: _____

Amount owed: $_____

Date of last charge: _____

Date of last payment: _____

Currently employed or active in business? _____

Bank: _____ Branch: _____

Debt is owed for: _____

Other Comments: _____

                             _____

STATE OF   }
COUNTY OF   }

On   before me,   , personally appeared   , personally known to me (or proved to me on the basis of satisfactory evidence) to be the person(s) whose name(s) is/are subscribed to the within instrument and acknowledged to me that he/she/they executed the same in his/her/their authorized capacity(ies), and that by his/her/their signature(s) on the instrument the person(s), or the entity upon behalf of which the person(s) acted, executed the instrument. WITNESS my hand and official seal.

Signature_____

                                    Affiant   _____Known   _____Unknown
                                    ID Produced_____
                                                      (Seal)

REFUSED CREDIT INFORMATION REQUEST

Date:

To:

Dear

    I have recently been declined credit by your firm on the transaction described below. In accordance with the Federal Fair Credit Reporting Act, I am requesting a full and complete disclosure of the reasons for this denial of credit and the nature of any adverse credit information received from any source other than a consumer reporting agency, including the identity of such source that submitted adverse credit information against me.

_____   _____
Signed   Full Name

_____   _____
Date of Credit Application   Address

_____   _____
Transaction or Type of Credit   Telephone Number

REJECTED GOODS NOTICE

Date:

To:

Dear

Please be advised that on _____, 19 , we received goods from you under our purchase order or contract dated _____, 19 .

We hereby notify you of our intent to reject and return said goods for the reason(s) checked below:

_____ Goods were not delivered within the time specified.

_____ Goods were defective or damaged as described on the reverse side.

_____ Goods were non-conforming to sample, advertisement, specifications, or price, as stated on the reverse side.

_____ Acknowledged acceptance of our order, as required, has not been received, and we therefore ordered these goods from other sources.

_____ Goods represent only a partial shipment and we will not accept back orders.

Please credit our account or issue a refund if prepaid, and provide instructions for return of said goods at your expense. Return of these goods however shall not be a waiver of any claim we may have under the Uniform Commercial Code or applicable law.

Very truly,

_____

Name

_____

Address

_____

RELEASE AND WAIVER OF OPTION RIGHTS

The undersigned is purchaser of an option to purchase and acquire real property dated
_____ , 19___ , executed by _____ as seller, and recorded on
_____ , 19___ , in volume _____ , on page _____ , of the deed records of
_____ County, State of _____ .

The option expired on _____ , 19___ .

Purchaser, the sole owner and holder of the option, acknowledges that the same was not exercised prior to the expiration date, and since that date the option has been and is now void and of no effect. Purchaser hereby waives and releases all claim, right, and interest in the option, and in the real property therein described.

IN WITNESS WHEREOF, this instrument has been executed on _____ ,
19___ .

_____

STATE OF _____ }
COUNTY OF _____

On _____ before me, _____ , personally appeared
_____ , personally known to me (or proved to me on the basis of satisfactory evidence) to be the person(s) whose name(s) is/are subscribed to the within instrument and acknowledged to me that he/she/they executed the same in his/her/their authorized capacity(ies), and that by his/her/their signature(s) on the instrument the person(s), or the entity upon behalf of which the person(s) acted, executed the instrument. WITNESS my hand and official seal.

Signature_____

Affiant _____Known _____Unknown
ID Produced_____
(Seal)

RELEASE OF BREACH OF LEASE BY TENANT

Acknowledgement made this   day of   , 19   , between
                    , (hereinafter "Landlord") and   ,
(hereinafter "Tenant").

Whereas, by a certain lease dated   day of   , 19   , and made
between Landlord and Tenant, all those premises described as:

were leased to the Tenant for the term of   years from the   day of   ,
19   , at the yearly rent thereby reserved, and subject to the Tenant's covenant therein contained,
including the following covenant:

; and

Whereas, a breach of the said covenant has been committed, to wit,
and the Landlord has agreed to execute such a release of the said breach.

Now, therefore, in consideration of $, receipt of which is acknowledged, the
Landlord waives and releases all existing rights and remedies for damages, forfeiture, or
otherwise which the Landlord has or could enforce against the Tenant for said breach or any
other breach hereto committed and ratified and confirms said lease; provided that this waiver and
release shall not extend to or prejudice any rights of the Landlord in respect of any future
breaches by the Tenant.

_____
Landlord

RELEASE OF MECHANIC'S LIENS

FOR GOOD CONSIDERATION, the undersigned contractor or subcontractor having furnished materials and/or labor for construction at the premises known as
, standing in the name of   ,
do hereby release all liens, or rights to file liens against said property for material and/or services or labor provided to this date, with it acknowledged however, that this discharge of lien shall not necessarily constitute a release or discharge of any claim for sums now or hereinafter due for said material and/or services, if existing.

This release shall be binding upon and inure to the benefit of the parties, their successors, assigns and personal representatives.

Signed this   day of   , 19   .

In the presence of:

_____
Company Name

_____   By:_____
Witness   Contractor/Subcontractor

_____
Address

_____

RELEASE OF MORTGAGE

The undersigned,   , of

, hereby certifies that the mortgage, dated   , 19   , executed by

, as mortgagor, to   , as mortgagee, and

recorded on   , 19   , in the office of the   of the County

of   , State of   , in the Book of Mortgages, page   ,

together with the debt secured by said mortgage, has been fully paid, satisfied, released, and

discharged, and that the property secured thereby has been released from the lien of such

mortgage.

IN WITNESS WHEREOF, the undersigned has executed this release on   ,

19   .

_____

STATE OF
COUNTY OF   }

On   before me,   , personally appeared
, personally known to me (or
proved to me on the basis of satisfactory evidence) to be the person(s) whose name(s) is/are
subscribed to the within instrument and acknowledged to me that he/she/they executed the same
in his/her/their authorized capacity(ies), and that by his/her/their signature(s) on the instrument
the person(s), or the entity upon behalf of which the person(s) acted, executed the instrument.
WITNESS my hand and official seal.
Signature_____

Affiant _____Known _____Unknown
ID Produced_____

(Seal)

RELEASE OF MORTGAGE BY A CORPORATION

            , a corporation incorporated under the laws of the State of   , having its principal office at   , hereby certifies that the mortgage, dated   , 19 , executed by   , as mortgagor, to   , as mortgagee, and recorded   , 19 , in the office of the   of the County of   , State of   , in the Book of mortgages, page   , together with the debt secured by said mortgage, has been fully paid, satisfied, released, and discharged, and that the property secured thereby has been released from the lien of such mortgage.

    IN WITNESS WHEREOF,   has caused this release to be duly signed by its   authorized to sign by the resolution of its board of directors and caused its corporate seal to be affixed hereto on   , 19 .

_____

Title:_____

STATE OF   }
COUNTY OF
On   before me,   , personally appeared   , personally known to me (or proved to me on the basis of satisfactory evidence) to be the person(s) whose name(s) is/are subscribed to the within instrument and acknowledged to me that he/she/they executed the same in his/her/their authorized capacity(ies), and that by his/her/their signature(s) on the instrument the person(s), or the entity upon behalf of which the person(s) acted, executed the instrument. WITNESS my hand and official seal.

Signature_____

Affiant   _____Known   _____Unknown
ID Produced_____
(Seal)

RELEASE—INDIVIDUAL

Release executed on   , 19 , by
(releasor) to   (releasee).

In consideration of   Dollars ($),
receipt of which is acknowledged, releasor voluntarily and knowingly executes this release with the express intention of effecting the extinguishment of obligations created by or arising out of:

Releasor, with the intention of binding itself, its spouse, heirs, legal representatives, and assigns, expressly releases and discharges releasee and its heirs and legal representatives from all claims, demands, actions, judgments, and executions that releasor ever had, or now has, or may have, known or unknown, against releasee or its heirs or legal representatives created by or arising out of said claim.

In witness whereof, releasor has executed this release on the day and year first above written.

                                        _____

RENEWAL OF FICTITIOUS OR ASSUMED NAME CERTIFICATE

CERTIFICATE

The undersigned hereby certify(ies) the following:

1. The undersigned, _____ , is or are conducting

a business at:

2. The most recent prior _____ name certificate was filed with _____ on

_____ , 19 _____ .

3. The true name(s) and residence(s) of each of the undersigned are:

4. This certificate reflects a change in the information set forth in the most recent prior

certificate.

This certificate is executed and filed as a renewal certificate pursuant to state law.

Date: _____   _____

                                         _____

STATE OF _____   }
COUNTY OF _____ }

On _____ before me, _____ , personally appeared
_____ , personally known to me (or
proved to me on the basis of satisfactory evidence) to be the person(s) whose name(s) is/are
subscribed to the within instrument and acknowledged to me that he/she/they executed the same
in his/her/their authorized capacity(ies), and that by his/her/their signature(s) on the instrument
the person(s), or the entity upon behalf of which the person(s) acted, executed the instrument.
WITNESS my hand and official seal.

Signature_____

                          Affiant _____Known _____Unknown
                          ID Produced_____
                                                    (Seal)

RENEWAL OF NOTICE OF ASSIGNMENT OF ACCOUNTS

Date:

To:

The notice of assignment of accounts receivable, File No.   , filed on the

day of   , 19   , naming   , as assignor and

, as assignee, is hereby renewed.

_____

REQUEST FOR BANK CREDIT REFERENCE

Date:

To:

Re:

Dear

    The above captioned account requested we obtain from you a banking reference. So that we may evaluate proper credit for the account, we would appreciate the following information:

1.   How long has the account maintained a banking relationship with you?

2.   What is the account's average balance?

3.   Does the account routinely overdraft?

4.   Is the account a borrowing or non-borrowing account?

5.   If the account borrows, please advise as to:

        Present balance on secured loans $

        Present balance on unsecured loans $

        Terms of repayment:

        Is repayment satisfactory?

6.   Are overall banking relationships satisfactory?

    Any additional comments or information you may provide would be greatly appreciated and, of course, we would equally appreciate any future information involving a change in the account's financial situation or its banking relations with you.

    All information shall be held in the strictest confidence.

                Very truly,

_____

REQUEST FOR CREDIT INTERCHANGE

Date:

To:

Re:

Dear

The above account has recently applied to our firm for credit and listed you as a credit reference. So that we may have adequate information on which to issue credit, we request the benefit of your credit experience with the account by providing us the following information:

High Credit: $

Low Credit: $

Terms:

How long sold:

Present balance owed: $

Payment history:

Any other credit information you believe helpful may be noted on the reverse side and shall be held strictly confidential. We are always pleased to reciprocate.

A stamped return envelope is enclosed for your convenience.

Very truly,

_____

REQUEST FOR CREDIT REPORT

Date:

To:

In accordance with the Federal Fair Credit Reporting Act, I hereby request a full and complete disclosure of my credit file. This should include both the sources of information on my file and the names and addresses of all parties who have received my credit report, whether in writing, orally or by other electronic means.

I enclose the sum of $ for this report.

Thank you for your cooperation.

_____   _____
Signature   Printed Full Name

_____   _____
Social Security Number   Address

_____   _____
Telephone Number   Prior or Other Names

    _____
Prior or Other Addresses

REQUEST FOR REFERENCE

Date:

To:

Re:

    The above-named individual has applied for a position with our company and indicates previous employment with your firm. The information requested below will help us to evaluate the applicant. We will hold your comments in strict confidence. Thank you for your cooperation.

Sincerely,

Personnel Department

Please Indicate:

Position With Your Firm:_____

Employed From_____Through_____

Final Salary $_____ Social Security No._____

Please rate the applicant on the basis of his employment with you (good/ fair/poor):

  Ability_____ Conduct_____ Attitude_____

  Efficiency _____ Attendance_____ Punctuality_____

What was the reason for termination?_____

_____

Would you re-hire? _____. If not, give reason:_____

_____

_____
Signature and Title

REQUEST UNDER FREEDOM OF INFORMATION ACT

Date:

To:

Dear

      Pursuant to the Federal Freedom of Information Act, I request disclosure of such information on me as may be maintained in your files, and to the extent said disclosure is required by law.

      Please forward said information to the address below.

      I appreciate your cooperation.

In the presence of:

_____

Witness

_____

Signature

_____

Name (Printed or Typed)

_____

Other Known Names

_____

Address

_____

_____

Social Security No.

RESERVATION OF CORPORATE NAME

Date:

To:

The undersigned,   of   ,
hereby applies for reservation of the following corporate name for a period of   days
following issuance of a certificate of reservation of corporate name.

Name to be reserved:

_____

RESERVATION OF MULTIPLE CORPORATE NAMES

Date:

To:

    The undersigned,

                    who are intended incorporators, hereby apply for reservation of the following corporate name for a period of   days:

    If the above name is unavailable for any reason, the undersigned request that one of the following corporate names be reserved, in the stated order of preference:

Second preference: _____

Third preference: _____

_____

_____

_____

RESIDENTIAL LEASE

LEASE AGREEMENT, entered into between

of   (Landlord) and   of

(Tenant).

For good consideration it is agreed between the parties as follows:

1.   Landlord hereby leases and lets to Tenant the premises described as follows:

2.   This Lease shall be for a term of   year(s), commencing on   , 19   ,

and terminating on   , 19   .

3.   Tenant shall pay Landlord the annual rent of $ during said term, in monthly

payments of $, each payable monthly on the first day of each month in advance. Tenant

shall pay a security deposit of $, to be returned upon termination of this Lease and the

payment of all rents due and performance of all other obligations.

4.   Tenant shall at its own expense provide the following utilities or services:

Landlord shall at its expense provide the following utilities or services:

5.   Tenant further agrees that:

> a)   Upon the expiration of the Lease it shall return possession of the leased premises
> in its present condition, reasonable wear and tear, fire casualty excepted. Tenant
> shall commit no waste to the leased premises.
>
> b)   Tenant shall not assign or sublet said premises or allow any other person to
> occupy the leased premises without Landlord's prior written consent.
>
> c)   Tenant shall not make any material or structural alterations to the leased premises
> without Landlord's prior written consent.
>
> d)   Tenant shall comply with all building, zoning and health codes and other
> applicable laws for the use of said leased premises.
>
> e)   Tenant shall not conduct on premises any activity deemed extra hazardous, or a
> nuisance, or requiring an increase in fire insurance premiums.
>
> f)   Tenant shall not allow pets on the premises.

g)   In the event of any breach of the payment of rent or any other allowed charge, or other breach of this Lease, Landlord shall have full rights to terminate this Lease in accordance with state law and re-enter and re-claim possession of the leased premises, in addition to such other remedies available to Landlord arising from said breach.

6.   This Lease shall be binding upon and inure to the benefit of the parties, their successors, assigns and personal representatives.

7.   This Lease shall be subordinate to all present or future mortgages against the property.

8.   Additional Lease terms:

Signed this   day of   , 19   .

In the presence of:

_____   _____
Witness   Landlord

_____   _____
Witness   Tenant

NOTICE: State law establishes rights and obligations for parties to rental agreements. This agreement is required to comply with the Truth in Renting Act or the applicable Landlord Tenant Statute or code of your state. If you have a question about the interpretation or legality of a provision of this agreement, you may want to seek assistance from a lawyer or other qualified person.

RESIDENTIAL RENTAL APPLICATION

Name of Applicant _____ Telephone_____

Present Address_____

City, State, Zip Code_____

Social Sec. No._____ Driver's Lic. No._____

Spouse's Social Sec. No._____ Spouse's Driver's Lic._____

    Birth Date_____ Spouse's Birth Date_____

    How many in your family? Adults_____ Children_____ Any Pets?_____

How long have you lived at the present address?_____

Name of Landlord_____Telephone_____

Prior Landlord_____Telephone_____

Employer_____Position_____

How long?_____ Telephone_____

Salary_____

Name of Bank_____

    _____ Checking   Account No._____

    _____ Savings   Account No._____

Additional Personal/Credit References

Name	Relationship	Telephone
_____	_____	_____
_____	_____	_____
_____	_____	_____

    I represent that the information provided in this application is true to the best of my knowledge. You are hereby authorized to verify my credit and employment references in connection with the processing of this application. I acknowledge receipt of a copy of this application.

Dated:

_____
Applicant

RESIGNATION

Date:

To:

Dear

    Please be advised that the undersigned hereby tenders this resignation as
                    , effective immediately. Please acknowledge receipt and acceptance of this resignation.

    Thank you for your cooperation.

               Very truly,

               _____
               Name

               _____
               Address

               _____

    The foregoing resignation is hereby accepted and is effective as of this   day of
         , 19   .

               _____
               Company

            By:_____

RESIGNATION OF TRUSTEE

Date:

To:

I,   , Trustee in the trust hereby give notice to you that I resign as Trustee to said trust. My resignation shall take effect on   . All my duties as trustee, except the duty to account, shall cease at such time.

_____

RETURN OF CLAIM AS NONCOLLECTIBLE

Date:

To:

Despite our repeated efforts, we have been unable to collect your claim against
. Since you have not authorized us to turn your accounts over to our
attorneys for litigation, we are returning this claim to you as noncollectible.

_____

REVOCABLE LIVING TRUST
Known as

_____

Date:

     Agreement made and executed this   day of   , 19   , by and between   , hereinafter referred to as the Grantor, and   , hereinafter referred to as the Trustee.

     Grantor desires to create a revocable trust of the property described in Schedule A hereto annexed, together with such monies, and other assets as the Trustee may hereafter at any time hold or acquire hereunder (hereinafter referred to collectively as the "Trust Estate") for the purposes hereinafter set forth.

     NOW, THEREFORE, in consideration of the premises and of the mutual covenants herein contained, the Grantor agrees to execute such further instruments as shall be necessary to vest the Trustee with full title to the property, and the Trustee agrees to hold the Trust Estate, IN TRUST, NEVERTHELESS, for the following uses and purposes and subject to the terms and conditions hereinafter set forth:

     The Trustee shall hold, manage, invest and reinvest the Trust Estate (if any requires such management and investment) and shall collect the income, if any, therefrom and shall dispose of the net income and principal as follows:

I

     (1)   During the lifetime of the Grantor, the Trustee shall pay to or apply for the benefit of the Grantor all the net income from the Trust.

     (2)   During the lifetime of the Grantor, the Trustee may pay to or apply for the benefit of the Grantor such sums from the principal of this Trust as in its sole discretion shall be necessary or advisable from time to time for the medical care, comfortable maintenance and welfare of the Grantor, taking into consideration to the extent the Trustee deems advisable, any other income or resources of the Grantor known to the Trustee.

     (3)   The Grantor may at any time during his/her lifetime and from time to time, withdraw all or any part of the principal of this Trust, free of trust, by delivering an instrument in writing duly signed by him/her to the Trustee, describing the property or portion thereof desired to be withdrawn. Upon receipt of such instrument, the Trustee shall thereupon convey and deliver to the Grantor, free of trust, the property described in such instrument.

     (4)   In the event that the Grantor is adjudicated to be incompetent or in the event that the Grantor is not adjudicated incompetent, but by reason of illness or mental or physical

disability is, in the opinion of the Trustee, unable to properly handle his/her own affairs, then and in that event the Trustee may during the Grantor's lifetime, in addition to the payments of income and principal for the benefit of the Grantor, pay to or apply for the benefit of the Grantor's spouse, and of any one or more of Grantor's minor children, such sums from the net income and from the principal of this Trust in such shares and proportions as in its sole discretion it shall determine to be necessary or advisable from time to time for the medical care, comfortable maintenance and welfare of the Grantor's said spouse and children taking into consideration to the extent the Trustee deems advisable, any other income or resources of the Grantor's said spouse and minor children known to the Trustee.

(5)   The interests of the Grantor shall be considered primary and superior to the interests of any beneficiary.

II

The Grantor reserves and shall have the exclusive right any time and from time to time during his/her lifetime by instrument in writing signed by the Grantor and delivered to the Trustee to modify or alter this Agreement, in whole or in part, without the consent of the Trustee or any beneficiary provided that the duties, powers and liabilities of the Trustee shall not be changed without his/her consent; and the Grantor reserves and shall have the right during his/her lifetime, by instrument in writing, signed by the Grantor and delivered to the Trustee, to cancel and annul this Agreement without the consent of the Trustee or any beneficiary hereof. Grantor expressly reserves the right to appoint successor trustees, replace present trustees and change the beneficiaries or the rights to property due any beneficiary.

III

In addition to any powers granted under applicable law or otherwise, and not in limitation of such powers, but subject to any rights and powers which may be reserved expressly by the Grantor in this Agreement, the Trustee is authorized to exercise the following powers to the Trustee's sole and absolute discretion.

a.   To hold and retain any or all property, real, personal, or mixed, received from the Grantor's estate, or from any other source, regardless of any law or rule of court relating to diversification, or non-productivity, for such time as the Trustee shall deem best, and to dispose of such property by sale, exchange, or otherwise, as and when they shall deem advisable; not withstanding this provision or any other contained herein.

b.   To sell, assign, exchange, transfer, partition and convey, or otherwise dispose of, any property, real, personal or mixed, which may be included in or may at any time become part of the Trust Estate, upon such terms and conditions as deemed advisable, at either public or private sale, including options and sales on credit and for the purpose of selling, assigning, exchanging, transferring, partitioning or conveying the same, to make, execute, acknowledge, and deliver any and all instruments of conveyance, deeds of trust, and assignments in such form and with such warranties and covenants as they may deem expedient and proper; and in the event of any sale, conveyance or other disposition of any of the Trust Estate, the purchaser shall not be obligated in any way to see the application of the purchase money or other consideration passing in connection therewith.

c.　　To lease or rent and manage any or all of the real estate, which may be included in or at any time become a part of the Trust Estate, upon such terms and conditions deemed advisable, irrespective of whether the term of the lease shall exceed the period permitted by law or the probable period of any trust created hereby, and to review and modify such leases; and for the purpose of leasing said real estate, to make, execute, acknowledge and deliver any and all instruments in such form and with such covenants and warranties as they may deem expedient and proper; and to make any repairs, replacements, and improvements, structural and otherwise, of any property, and to charge the expense thereof in an equitable manner to principal or income, as deemed proper.

d.　　To borrow money for any purpose in connection with said Trust created hereby, and to execute promissory notes or other obligations for amounts so borrowed, and to secure the payment of any such amounts by mortgage or pledge or any real or personal property, and to renew or extend the time of payment of any obligation, secured or unsecured, payable to or by any trust created hereby, for such periods of time as deemed advisable.

e.　　To invest and reinvest or leave temporarily uninvested any or all of the funds of the Trust Estate as said Trustee in the Trustee's sole discretion may deem best, including investments in stocks, common and preferred, and common trust fund, without being restricted to those investments expressly approved by statute for investment by fiduciaries, and to change investments from realty to personality, and vice versa.

f.　　To compromise, adjust, arbitrate, sue or defend, abandon, or otherwise deal with and settle claims, in favor of or against the Trust Estate as the Trustee shall deem best and the Trustee's decision shall be conclusive.

g.　　To determine in a fair and reasonable manner whether any part of the Trust Estate, or any addition or increment thereto be income or principal, or whether any cost, charge, expense, tax, or assessment shall be charged against income or principal, or partially against income and partially against principal.

h.　　To engage and compensate, out of principal or income or both, as equitably determined, agents, accountants, brokers, attorneys-in-fact, attorneys-at-law, tax specialists, realtors, custodians, investment counsel, and other assistants and advisors, and to do so without liability for any neglect, omission, misconduct, or default of any such agent or professional representative, provided he or she was selected and retained with reasonable care.

i.　　To vote any stock, bonds, or other securities held by the Trust at any meetings of stockholders, bondholders, or other security holders and to delegate the power so to vote to attorneys-in-fact or proxies under power of attorney, restricted or unrestricted, and to join in or become party to any organization, readjustment, voting trust, consideration or exchange, and to deposit securities with any persons, and to pay any fees incurred in connection therewith, and to charge the same to principal or income, as deemed proper, and to exercise all of the rights with regard to such securities.

j.　　To purchase securities, real estate, or other property from the executor or other personal representative of the Grantor's estate, the executor or other personal representative of the Grantor's spouse's estate, and the Trustees of any agreement or declaration executed by the Grantor during his/her lifetime under his/her last will in case his/her executors or Trustees are in need of cash, liquid assets, or income-producing assets with which to pay taxes, claims, or other estate or trust indebtedness, or in case such executors or Trustees are in need of such property to properly exercise and discharge their discretion with respect to distributions to beneficiaries as provided for under such bills, declarations, or agreements. Such purchase may be in cash or may be in exchange for other property of this Trust, and the Trustees shall not be liable in any way for any loss resulting to the Trust Estate by reason of the exercise of said authority.

k.   To undertake such further acts as are incidental to any of the foregoing or are reasonably required to carry out the tenor, purpose and intent of the Trust.

l.   To make loans or advancements to the executor or other personal representative of the Grantor's estate, the executor or other personal representative of the Grantor's spouse's estate, and the Trustees of any agreement or declaration executed by the Grantor during his/her lifetime or under his/her last will in case such executors or Trustees are in need of cash for any reason. Such loans or advancements may be secured or unsecured, and the Trustees shall not be liable in any way for any loss resulting to the Trust Estate by reason of the exercise of this authority.

IV

Upon death of the Grantor, or the last surviving Grantor if more than one, the remaining Trust assets shall be distributed to the beneficiaries in the proportionate or allocable amounts as are specified in the schedule of beneficiaries as may then be in force.

If any beneficiary and the Grantor should die under such circumstances as would render it doubtful whether the beneficiary or the Grantor died first, then it shall be conclusively presumed for the purposes of this Trust that said beneficiary predeceased the Grantor.

V

If it shall be determined that any provision of the Trust created herein violates any rule against perpetuities or remoteness of vesting now or hereafter in effect in a governing jurisdiction, that portion of the Trust herein created shall be administered as herein provided until the termination of the maximum period allowed by law at which time and forthwith such part of the Trust shall be distributed in fee simple to the beneficiaries then entitled to receive income therefrom, and for the purpose, it shall be presumed that any beneficiary entitled to receive support or education from the income or principal of any particular fund is entitled to receive the income therefrom.

VI

Except as otherwise provided herein, all payments of principal and income payable, or to become payable, to the beneficiary of any trust created hereunder shall not be subject to anticipation, assignment, pledge, sale or transfer in any manner, nor shall any said beneficiary have the power to anticipate or encumber such interest, nor shall such interest, while in possession of the Trustee, be liable for, or subject to, the debts, contracts, obligations, liabilities or torts of any beneficiary.

VII

This Trust Agreement shall be construed, regulated and governed by and in accordance with the laws of the State of   .

I certify that I have read the foregoing Trust Agreement and that it correctly states the terms and conditions under which the Trust Estate is to be held, managed and disposed of by the Trustee.

Dated:

_____
Grantor

_____
Trustee

WITNESSES:

The grantor has signed this trust at the end and has declared or signified in our presence that it is his/her revocable living trust, and in the presence of the Grantor and each other we have hereunto subscribed our names this   day of   , 19   .

_____   _____
Witness Signature   Address

_____   _____
Witness Signature   Address

_____   _____
Witness Signature   Address

We,_____, _____,

_____, and_____, the grantor and

the witnesses, respectively, whose names are signed to the attached and foregoing instrument

were sworn and declared to the undersigned that the Grantor signed the instrument as his/her revocable living trust and that each of the witnesses, in the presence of the Grantor and each other, signed the trust as witnesses.

Grantor: _____   Witness:_____

Witness:_____

Witness:_____

STATE OF _____ }
COUNTY OF _____

On _____ before me, _____ ,personally appeared, _____ Grantor, _____ ,witness, _____ , witness,_____ ,witness personally known to me (or proved to me on the basis of satisfactory evidence) to be the person(s) whose name(s) is/are subscribed to the within instrument and acknowledged to me that he/she/they executed the same in his/her/their authorized capacity(ies), and that by his/her/their signature(s) on the instrument the person(s), or the entity upon behalf of which the person(s) acted, executed the instrument. WITNESS my hand and official seal.

Signature_____   Affiant ___Known ___Produced ID
          Notary Public   ID Produced _____
                                                                (Seal)

NOTE: A living trust may be used for any estate. However, if your gross estate (including living trust property) now or in the future, exceeds $600,000 ($1,200,000 for a married couple), consult an attorney. You may want to consider options such as a credit shelter trust.

REVOCABLE PROXY

BE IT KNOWN, that the undersigned,   of

                    , being the owner of   shares of voting common stock

of   (Corporation), does hereby grant to   ,

a proxy to vote on my behalf   shares of stock at any future general or special meeting of

the stockholders of the Corporation. Said proxy-holder is entitled to attend said meetings on my

behalf or vote said shares through mail proxy, all to the same extent as if I voted said shares

personally, and may vote on any matter that may properly come before said stockholder meeting.

During the pendency of this proxy, all rights to vote said shares shall be held by the

proxy-holder and shall not be voted by the Undersigned, provided the undersigned may revoke

this proxy at any time, upon written notice of termination by certified mail, return receipt.

The proxy-holder shall be entitled to reimbursement for reasonable expenses incurred

hereunder, but otherwise shall not be entitled to compensation for the services to be rendered.

This agreement shall be binding upon and inure to the benefit of the parties, their

successors, assigns, and personal representatives.

Signed under seal this   day of   , 19   .

_____

STATE OF   }
COUNTY OF

On   before me,   , personally appeared
                                        , personally known to me (or
proved to me on the basis of satisfactory evidence) to be the person(s) whose name(s) is/are
subscribed to the within instrument and acknowledged to me that he/she/they executed the same
in his/her/their authorized capacity(ies), and that by his/her/their signature(s) on the instrument
the person(s), or the entity upon behalf of which the person(s) acted, executed the instrument.
WITNESS my hand and official seal.

Signature_____

                                        Affiant   _____Known   _____Unknown

ID Produced_____

(Seal)

REVOCATION OF GUARANTY

Date:

To:

    Reference is made to our guaranty dated   , 19   , issued to you by the undersigned guaranteeing the continued credit of   (Obligor).

    Please be advised that effective upon receipt of this letter of guaranty (or such effective date as provided under the guaranty), the undersigned shall not be obligated under the guaranty for any future or further credit extended by you to the Obligor. We understand that we shall remain liable for the present balance until paid.

    We would appreciate confirmation of the present balance owed and would further appreciate notification when said balance has been fully paid.

    Please confirm to us in writing receipt and acknowledgement of this guaranty revocation by return acknowledgement below.

    Thank you for your cooperation.

Very truly,

_____

Acknowledged:

_____

Effective Date:_____

REVOCATION OF POWER OF ATTORNEY

To:

I hereby make reference to a certain power of attorney granted by me,

, as principal, to you, , as my Attorney-in-Fact, and

dated , 19 .

This document acknowledges that as principal I hereby revoke, rescind and terminate

said power-of-attorney and all authority, rights and power thereto effective this date.

Please acknowledge receipt of this revocation and return said acknowledged copy to me.

Signed under seal this day of , 19 .

_____
Grantor

STATE OF
COUNTY OF }

On before me, , personally appeared
, personally known to me (or
proved to me on the basis of satisfactory evidence) to be the person(s) whose name(s) is/are
subscribed to the within instrument and acknowledged to me that he/she/they executed the same
in his/her/their authorized capacity(ies), and that by his/her/their signature(s) on the instrument
the person(s), or the entity upon behalf of which the person(s) acted, executed the instrument.
WITNESS my hand and official seal.

Signature_____

Affiant _____Known _____Unknown
ID Produced_____
(Seal)

Acknowledged:

_____
Attorney-in-Fact

REVOCATION OF PROXY

I, _____ , the holder of _____ shares of common voting stock of _____ (Corporation), having appointed _____ to act as my proxy by a written proxy dated _____ , 19____ , a copy of which is attached, do hereby revoke that proxy.

IN WITNESS WHEREOF, I do hereby execute this revocation of proxy in duplicate on this, the _____ day of _____ , 19____ . The original of this revocation shall be filed in the office of the _____ Corporation, and the duplicate copy of this revocation shall be delivered by Certified Mail, Return Receipt Requested, to _____ , the person named by me as my proxy in the revoked proxy agreement.

_____

STATE OF _____
COUNTY OF _____ }

On _____ before me, _____ , personally appeared _____ , personally known to me (or proved to me on the basis of satisfactory evidence) to be the person(s) whose name(s) is/are subscribed to the within instrument and acknowledged to me that he/she/they executed the same in his/her/their authorized capacity(ies), and that by his/her/their signature(s) on the instrument the person(s), or the entity upon behalf of which the person(s) acted, executed the instrument. WITNESS my hand and official seal.

Signature_____

Affiant _____Known _____Unknown
ID Produced_____
(Seal)

SALE ON APPROVAL
ACKNOWLEDGEMENT

Date:

To:

We acknowledge the goods delivered on the attached invoice or order were sold on a sale-on-approval basis.

In the event you are not satisfied with the goods you have the right to return all or any part thereof at our expense within _____ days of receipt for full credit (or refund if prepaid).

Goods not returned within that time shall be deemed accepted, and there shall be no further right of return.

We thank you for your business and hope the goods will prove satisfactory and meet with your approval.

Very truly,

_____

SALES REPRESENTATIVE AGREEMENT

Agreement between   (Company) and

(Sales Representative).

Sales Representative agrees to:

1. Represent and sell the Company's   products/services in the geographic area of

2. Accurately represent and state Company policies to all potential and present customers.

3. Promptly mail in all leads and orders to the Company.

4. Inform the sales manager of all problems concerning Company customers within the sales territory.

5. Inform the sales manager if the Sales Representative is representing, or plans to represent any other business firm. In no event shall sales representative represent a competitive company or product line either within or outside the designated sales area.

6. Telephone the Company with reasonable frequency to discuss sales activity within the territory.

7. Provide company 30-days' notice should the Representative intend to terminate this agreement.

8. Return promptly all materials and samples provided by the Company to the Representative, if either party terminates this agreement.

The Company Agrees to:

1. Pay the following commissions to the Sales Representative:

   (a)   percent of all prepaid sales, except as stated in (4) below

   (b)   percent of all credit sales, except as stated in (4) below

2. To negotiate in advance of sale the commission percentage to be paid on all orders that the Company allows a quantity discount or other trade concession.

3. Commissions on refunds to customers or merchandise returned by the customer in which a commission has already been paid to the Representative shall be deducted from future commissions to be paid to the Representative by the Company.

4. Except by special arrangement, the following shall not be commissioned:

5. To provide the Sales Representative with reasonable quantities of business cards, brochures, catalogs, and any product samples required for sales purposes.

6. To set minimum monthly quotas after consultation with the Sales Representative.

7. To grant Representative 30-days' notice should the Company wish to terminate this agreement.

8. To pay commissions to the Representative on sales from existing customers for a period of   (   ) months after this agreement is terminated by either party.

9. This constitutes the entire agreement.

10. This agreement shall be binding upon the parties and their successors and assigns.

Signed this   day of   , 19   .

_____   _____
Company   Sales Representative

SECOND NOTICE OF OVERDUE ACCOUNT

Date:

To:

Dear

      There can be no better way to show you why we are concerned about your overdue account than to list your account balance.

PAST DUE

Over 30 Days	$_____
Over 60 days	$_____
Over 90 days	$_____
Total	$_____

May we now have your check without further delay.

Very truly,

_____

SECURITY AGREEMENT

Date:

BE IT KNOWN, that for good consideration

of _____ (Debtor) grants to

of _____ and its successors and assigns

(Secured Party) a security interest pursuant to Article 9 of the Uniform Commercial Code in the following property (Collateral), which shall include all after-acquired property of a like nature and description and proceeds and products thereof:

This security interest is granted to secure payment and performance on the following obligations as well as all other debts now or hereinafter owed Secured Party from Debtor:

Debtor hereby acknowledges to Secured Party that:

1.   The collateral shall be kept at the Debtor's above address and not moved or relocated without written consent.

2.   The Debtor warrants that Debtor owns the collateral and it is free from any other lien, encumbrance and security interest or adverse interest and the Debtor has full authority to grant this security interest.

3.   Debtor agrees to execute such financing statements as are reasonably required by Secured Party to perfect this security agreement in accordance with state law and the Uniform Commercial Code.

4.   Upon default in payment or performance of any obligation for which this security interest

is granted, or breach of any term of this security agreement, then in such instance Secured Party may declare all obligations immediately due and payable and shall have all remedies of a secured party under the Uniform Commercial Code, as enacted in the Debtor's state, which rights shall be cumulative and not necessarily successive with any other rights or remedies.

5.   Debtor agrees to maintain such insurance coverage on the collateral as Secured Party may from time to time reasonably require and Secured Party shall be named as loss payee.

6.   This security agreement shall further be in default upon the death, insolvency or bankruptcy of any party who is an obligor to this agreement or upon any material decrease in the value of the collateral or adverse change in the financial condition of the Debtor.

7.   Upon default the Debtor shall pay all reasonable attorneys' fees and costs of collection necessary to enforce this agreement.

IN WITNESS WHEREOF, this agreement is signed this   day of   ,
19   .

_____
Debtor

_____
Secured Party

Note: Record this security agreement or financing statements in appropriate filing office to protect your rights against third parties.

SIGHT DRAFT

Date:

To:

Dear

     Upon presentment, you are directed to debit our account and pay to the order of

the sum of

Dollars ($).

_____
Account Name

By:_____
Authorized Signature

_____
Account Number

SPECIFIC GUARANTY

FOR GOOD AND VALUABLE CONSIDERATION, and as an inducement for

of   (Creditor), to

extend credit to   of   (Borrower);

the undersigned jointly, severally and unconditionally guarantee to Creditor the prompt and full

payment of the following obligation:

And the undersigned agree to remain bound on this guaranty notwithstanding any

extension, renewal, indulgence, forbearance or waiver, or release, discharge or substitution of

any collateral or security for the obligation. In the event of default, the Creditor may seek

payment directly from the undersigned without need to proceed first against Borrower, and the

undersigned waive all suretyship defenses.

The obligations of the undersigned under this guarantee shall be only to the specific debt

described and to no other debt or obligation between Borrower and Creditor.

In the event of default, the guarantor shall be responsible for all attorneys' fees and

reasonable costs of collection.

This guaranty shall be binding upon and inure to the benefit of the parties, their

successors, assigns and personal representatives.

Signed this   day of   , 19   .

In the Presence of:

_____   _____
Witness   Creditor

_____   _____
Witness   Borrower

SPECIFIC POWER OF ATTORNEY

BE IT ACKNOWLEDGED, that I,   of
                                        , the undersigned, do hereby grant a limited and specific power of attorney to   of
                          , as my attorney-in-fact.

Said attorney-in-fact shall have full power and authority to undertake and perform only the following acts on my behalf:

The authority herein shall include such incidental acts as are reasonably required to carry out and perform the specific authorities granted herein.

My attorney-in-fact agrees to accept this appointment subject to its terms, and agrees to act and perform in said fiduciary capacity consistent with my best interest as he/she in his/her discretion deems advisable.

This power of attorney is effective upon execution. This power of attorney may be revoked by me at any time, and shall automatically be revoked upon my death, provided any person relying on this power of attorney shall have full rights to accept and rely upon the authority of my attorney-in-fact until in receipt of actual notice of revocation.

Signed this   day of   , 19   .

_____   _____
Witness   Grantor

_____   _____
Witness   Attorney-in Fact

STATE OF
COUNTY OF   }

On   before me,   , personally appeared
                                                    , personally known to me (or proved to me on the basis of satisfactory evidence) to be the person(s) whose name(s) is/are subscribed to the within instrument and acknowledged to me that he/she/they executed the same in his/her/their authorized capacity(ies), and that by his/her/their signature(s) on the instrument the person(s), or the entity upon behalf of which the person(s) acted, executed the instrument. WITNESS my hand and official seal.

Signature_____

                              Affiant   _____Known   _____Unknown
                              ID Produced_____
                                                                      (Seal)

SPECIFIC RELEASE

BE IT KNOWN, for good consideration, the undersigned

of

jointly and severally hereby forever release, discharge and acquit

of   ,

from any and all contracts, claims, suits, actions or liabilities both in law and in equity

specifically arising from, relating to or otherwise described as and limited to:

This release applies only to the foregoing matters and extends to no other debt, account, agreement, obligations, cause of action, liability or undertaking by and between the parties, which, if existing, shall survive this release and remain in full force and effect and undisturbed by this specific release.

This release shall be binding upon and inure to the benefit of the parties, their successors, assigns and personal representatives.

Signed this   day of   , 19   .

Witnessed:

_____   _____
Witness   First Party

_____   _____
Witness   Second Party

STATEMENT OF WISHES

OF

_____

I, _____ , do hereby set forth certain wishes and requests to my personal representatives, heirs, family, friends and others who may carry out these wishes. I understand these wishes are advisory only and not mandatory.

My wishes are:

Dated:

_____
Signature

STOCK SUBSCRIPTION

I,   , the undersigned do hereby subscribe for the purchase of (   ) shares of the common stock of

            (Corporation), for the aggregate purchase price of $. I understand that upon issue, said shares shall constitute   % of the common shares outstanding and entitled to vote and that there are no other shares outstanding.

_____

The foregoing subscription is accepted and the Treasurer shall issue said shares upon payment to the corporation the sum of $.

_____
For the Corporation
and its Board of Directors

STOCK TRANSFER

FOR VALUE RECEIVED, the undersigned

of   hereby sells, assigns and transfers to

of

and its successors and assigns, (   ) shares of the   stock of

, represented by Certificate No(s).   , inclusive, standing in the

name of the undersigned in the books of said company.

The undersigned also hereby irrevocably constitutes and appoints

, attorney-in-fact, to transfer the said stock on the books of said company with

full power of substitution in the premises.

Signed this   day of   , 19   .

Witnessed:

_____   _____
Witness   Signature Guaranteed

STOCKHOLDERS REDEMPTION AGREEMENT

Agreement made this   day of   , 19   , between

                    , a corporation incorporated under the laws of the State of

with its principal place of business at:

(hereinafter "Corporation") and   (hereinafter "Stockholder").

RECITALS

A. Stockholder is the owner of   shares of the common stock of Corporation.

B. Corporation desires to redeem all of said shares upon the terms and conditions set forth below.

C. Stockholder is willing that said shares be redeemed on the terms and conditions set forth below.

D. Stockholder desires that such redemption shall be accorded capital gains, rather than ordinary income treatment, under the rules imposed by the Internal Revenue Code, as implemented by the regulations adopted pursuant thereto.

E. It is necessary that all the shares held by the Stockholder shall be redeemed, and that certain other conditions be met in order for Stockholder to be entitled said income tax benefits.

In consideration of the mutual covenants and agreements herein contained, the parties mutually agree to the following:

1. PAYMENT TO STOCKHOLDER. On the aforesaid date, Corporation will pay to stockholder the sum of

Dollars ($) for said shares of the common capital stock of Corporation.

2. SURRENDER OF CERTIFICATES. On the aforesaid date, Stockholder will surrender to Corporation the certificates representing all such shares of stock, which certificates shall be duly endorsed.

3. RESIGNATION OF STOCKHOLDER. Stockholder hereby tenders his resignation as director, officer, and employee of Corporation, all of which resignations shall be presented to the

Board of Directors of Corporation and which shall be effective immediately upon the execution of this agreement.

4. LIMITATIONS ON STOCKHOLDER AFTER TERMINATION. Stockholder will not acquire any stock, other than by gift, bequest, or inheritance, in corporation within _____ years from the date hereof, nor will stockholder be a director or otherwise employed in any corporation within that period.

IN WITNESS WHEREOF, the parties have executed this agreement on the day and year first above written.

_____   _____

Witness   Stockholder

_____   _____

Witness

                              By:_____

                              Title:_____

SUBLEASE

Sublease agreement entered into between   of

                    (Tenant),   of

(Subtenant) and   of

(Landlord).

Sublease Period: The Subtenant agrees to sublease from Tenant, property known as

                                            from   , 19   , to

     , 19   .

Terms of Sublease: The Subtenant agrees to comply with all terms and conditions of the

lease entered into by the Tenant, including the prompt payment of all rents. The lease terms are

incorporated into this agreement by reference. The Subtenant agrees to pay the Landlord the

monthly rent stated in that lease, and all other rental charges hereinafter due, and otherwise

assume all of Tenant's obligations during the Sublease period and to indemnify Tenant from any

liability arising from subtenant's breach.

Security Deposit: The Subtenant agrees to pay to Tenant the sum of $

as a security deposit, to be promptly returned upon the termination of this sublease and

compliance of all conditions of this sublease.

Inventory: Attached to this agreement is an inventory of items or fixtures on the above

described property on   , 19   . The Subtenant agrees to replace or

reimburse the Tenant for any of these items that are missing or damaged.

Landlord's Consent: The Landlord consents to this sublease and agrees to promptly notify the Tenant at

if the Subtenant is in breach of this agreement. Nothing herein shall constitute a release of Tenant who shall remain bound under this lease. Nothing herein shall constitute a consent to any further Sublease or Assignment of Lease.

Date:

_____
Landlord

_____
Subtenant

_____
Tenant

SURETY BOND

Surety bond by   as principal, and

as surety, a corporation incorporated under the laws of the State of   ,   and

licensed to transact a surety business in the State of   , to

                        , as obligee.

RECITALS

A. Principal and surety are bound to obligee in the sum of   Dollars

($), for the payment of which principal and surety jointly and severally bind

themselves, their successors, assigns, and legal representatives.

B. Principal and obligee have entered into a written contract for

(hereinafter "contract") which was executed on   , 19   , a copy of which is

attached and incorporated by reference.

1. DURATION. This obligation shall run continuously and shall remain in full force and

effect until and unless the bond is terminated and cancelled as provided herein or as otherwise

provided by law.

2. CONDITION OF OBLIGATION. If principal fully performs its obligation or

indemnifies obligee against any loss resulting from the breach of any part of the original contract

by principal, this obligation shall be void.

3. NOTICE. No liability shall attach to surety hereunder unless upon discovery of any

fact or circumstance indicating a possible claim hereunder, immediate written notice thereof

containing all details then known is given to surety at its principal office at:

4. TERMINATION. Surety may terminate its obligation by giving written notice to

obligee, but such notice shall not affect any obligation which may have arisen prior to the receipt

of such notice by obligee.

5. COMPLETION OF ORIGINAL CONTRACT: SUBROGATION. In case of default by

principal, surety may assure and complete or procure completion of the obligations of principal,

and surety shall be subrogated and entitled to all the rights and properties of principal arising out

of the original contract.

6. EXTENT OF LIABILITY. The maximum amount of the liability of surety shall be no more than _____ Dollars ($ _____), together with the interest due thereon.

7. MODIFICATION OF ORIGINAL CONTRACT. Any modification in the obligations of the original contract may be made without the consent or knowledge of surety and without in any way releasing surety from liability under this bond.

8. SEVERABILITY. If any of the provisions of this bond are held to be illegal or unenforceable by a court of competent jurisdiction, all other provisions shall remain effective.

9. BINDING EFFECT. This bond shall be binding and inure on surety and its successors, assigns, and legal representatives.

IN WITNESS WHEREOF, principal and surety have executed this bond on _____ , 19 ___ .

_____   _____
Principal   Surety

TENANT'S NOTICE TO EXERCISE PURCHASE OPTION

Date:

To:

Dear

     Notice is hereby provided that the undersigned as Lessee under a certain Lease dated

            , 19   , does hereby exercise its purchase option under said lease to

purchase the property described as

for the option price of $.

     As contained within the lease agreement I enclose $ as a deposit toward said

purchase option.

_____

Lessee

CERTIFIED MAIL, Return Receipt Requested

TENANT'S NOTICE TO TERMINATE TENANCY

Date:

To:

Please be advised that as your tenant on certain premises described as:

we hereby notify you of our intention to terminate our tenancy effective   , 19   .
On or before said date, we shall deliver to you full possession of the premises, together with the keys, and if applicable we request prompt return of any security deposit or escrow that you may be holding.

Thank you for your cooperation.

_____
Tenant

_____
Address

_____

CERTIFIED MAIL, Return Receipt Requested

THREE DAY NOTICE TO VACATE
FOR NON-PAYMENT OF RENT

Date:

To:

    Notice to you and all others in possession, that you are hereby notified to quit and deliver up the premises you hold as our tenant, namely:

    You are to deliver up said premises on or within three days of receipt of this notice.

    This notice is provided due to non-payment of rent. The present rent arrearage is in the amount of $_____. You may redeem your tenancy by full payment of said arrears within three days as provided under the terms of your tenancy or by state law. In the event you fail to bring your rent payments current or vacate the premises we shall immediately take legal action to evict you and to recover all damages due us for the unlawful detention of said premises.

_____
Landlord

CERTIFIED MAIL, Return Receipt Requested

TIME NOTE

FOR VALUE RECEIVED, the undersigned promise to pay to the order of

, the sum of

Dollars ($), payable with annual interest of   % on any unpaid balance.

All principal and accrued interest shall be fully due and payable on   ,

19   , time being of the essence.

This note may be prepaid, in whole or in part, without penalty.

All parties to this note waive presentment, demand, protest or notices thereto and agree to remain bound notwithstanding any indulgence, modification or release or discharge of any party or collateral securing this note. The undersigned shall be jointly and severally liable under this note.

Upon default, the undersigned agree to pay all reasonable attorneys' fees and costs of collection.

Signed this   day of   , 19   .

Signed in the presence of:

_____   _____
Witness   Maker

_____   _____
Witness   Maker

TRIP PERMISSION

The undersigned _____, referred to as Parent, is the parent and lawful guardian of _____, a minor.

Parent acknowledges that said minor is authorized to take the following trip _____, sponsored by _____, and to engage in all activities incident thereto.

Parent hereby appoints _____ as *loco parentis*, and is authorized to render such emergency medical care to _____ as could be undertaken by the parent, and the parent hereby releases said _____, and its agents and employees from any and all acts taken in good faith during the trip.

Signed this _____ day of _____, 19____.

In the presence of:

_____   _____
Witness   Parent

UNSOLICITED IDEA ACKNOWLEDGEMENT

To:

Dear

We appreciate your interest in submitting for our consideration an idea or proposal relative to:

Our company receives many commercial ideas, suggestions and proposals, and also has many of its own projects under development or consideration. Therefore, it is possible the idea or proposal you plan to submit to us has been considered and/or may already be in the planning or development stages.

Therefore, we would be pleased to accept your idea or proposal for consideration provided you acknowledge:

1.   Samples or other submissions will be returned only if return postage or freight is prepaid.

2.   The company accepts no responsibility for casualty or loss to samples or other submitted material in our possession.

3.   The company accepts no responsibility for holding any submitted information in confidence, but shall use its best efforts to hold it confidential.

4.   The company shall pay compensation only in the event it a) accepts the submitted idea, b) has received the idea only from you, and c) reaches agreement with you as to terms and conditions.

5.   Company agrees not to exploit said idea, directly or indirectly, without first entering into a compensation agreement acceptable to you.

6.   Nothing in this agreement shall be deemed to give company any rights in the materials submitted.

7.   Company shall have no obligation to you in the event this idea or material is presently under consideration by company.

If these terms are acceptable to you, please sign where indicated below and submit with your idea or proposal.

_____

The foregoing terms and conditions are understood and acknowledged this

day of   , 19   .

In the presence of:

_____   _____
Witness   Submitter

VERIFICATION OF EDUCATION

Date:

To:

Re:

The above individual has applied to our organization for employment.

According to the information in the employment application, this individual has attended your school. Would you please verify the above by completing the following information:

Dates Attended:_____

Still Attending? _____

Degree/Diploma Earned: _____

Grade Point Average:___ _____

Honors or Commendations: _____

Other Comments:_____

_____

Your cooperation in completing and returning this in the self-enclosed envelope is greatly appreciated.

Very truly,

_____

VERIFICATION OF LICENSURE

Date:

To:

    Please be advised that as a condition of my employment with   ,

I hereby authorize release of information relative to the status of my license or registration as a

within the state of   .

Please certify below and return to:

Firm   _____

Address   _____

           _____

Attn: _____

           Thank you.

_____

CERTIFICATION

    This will certify that the above,   , is duly licensed in the State of

        as a   , and said license, or registration is

in good standing with no disciplinary or revocation proceedings pending.

Dated:

_____
Certifying Official

WAIVER AND ASSUMPTION OF RISK

The undersigned, _____ (Customer), voluntarily makes and grants this Waiver and Assumption of Risk in favor of _____ (Seller) as partial consideration (in addition to monies paid to Seller for the opportunity to use the facilities, equipment, materials and/or other assets of Seller; and/or to receive assistance, training, guidance, tutelage and/or instruction from the personnel of Seller; and/or to engage in the activities, events, sports, festivities and/or gatherings sponsored by Seller; I do hereby waive and release any and all claims whether in contract or of personal injury, bodily injury, property damage, damages, losses and/or death that may arise from my aforementioned use or receipt, as I understand and recognize that there are certain risks, dangers and perils connected with such use and/or receipt, which I hereby acknowledge have been fully explained to me and which I fully understand, and which I nevertheless accept, assume and undertake after inquiry and investigation of extent, duration, and completeness wholly satisfactory and acceptable to me. I further agree to use my best judgment in undertaking these activities, use and/or receipt and to faithfully adhere to all safety instructions and recommendations, whether oral or written. I hereby certify that I am a competent adult assuming these risks of my own free will, being under no compulsion or duress. This Waiver and Assumption of Risk is effective from _____ , 19 ___ , to _____ , 19 ___ , inclusive, and may not be revoked, altered, amended, rescinded or voided without the express prior written consent of Seller.

_____
Print Name

_____
Customer's Signature

_____
Address

_____
Date

_____
Age

WAIVER OF LIEN

KNOW ALL MEN BY THESE PRESENTS: That

for and in consideration of   Dollars ($)

and other good and valuable consideration, to be paid, the receipt whereof is hereby

acknowledged, do hereby waive, release, remise and relinquish any and all right to claim any

lien or liens for work done or material furnished, or any kind of class of lien whatsoever on the

following described property:

Title owner of said property: _____

Signed, sealed and dated this   day of   , 19   at

Signed in the presence of:

_____   By:_____

Witness

STATE OF

COUNTY OF   }

On   before me,   , personally appeared

                                   , personally known to me (or

proved to me on the basis of satisfactory evidence) to be the person(s) whose name(s) is/are
subscribed to the within instrument and acknowledged to me that he/she/they executed the same
in his/her/their authorized capacity(ies), and that by his/her/their signature(s) on the instrument
the person(s), or the entity upon behalf of which the person(s) acted, executed the instrument.
WITNESS my hand and official seal.

Signature_____

                               Affiant   _____Known   _____Unknown

                               ID Produced_____

                                                    (Seal)

WAIVER OF NOTICE—COMBINED MEETING

I, the undersigned, the holder of   shares of stock of

and/or a Board of Director, do hereby waive notice of the combined meeting of shareholders and

board of directors of the said corporation.

Furthermore, the undersigned hereby agrees that said meeting shall be held at   .m. on

          , 19   , at the following location:

Date: _____

WAIVER OF NOTICE OF ANNUAL MEETING
BY INDIVIDUAL SHAREHOLDER

I, the undersigned, the holder of   shares of stock of

do hereby waive notice of the annual meeting of shareholders of the

Corporation which will be held for the following purposes:

(1)   Electing a new board of directors.

(2)   Transacting any other business that may properly be brought before the meeting.

The undersigned hereby consents to the holding of the meeting on   ,

19   , at   .m. at the offices of the Corporation which are located at

, in the City of

Date: _____   _____

WAIVER OF NOTICE OF DIRECTORS' MEETING

The undersigned, constituting the entire membership of the Board of Directors of
, hereby waive notice of the meeting of the
Board of Directors of the Corporation and consent to the holding of the meeting at   .m. on
, 19   , at the offices of the Corporation located at
. Furthermore, we agree that any lawful business
may be transacted at the meeting.

Dated:

_____

_____

_____

WAIVER OF NOTICE OF ORGANIZATION
MEETING OF INCORPORATORS AND DIRECTORS

OF_____

    We do hereby constitute the Incorporators and Directors of the above captioned Corporation and do hereby waive notice of the organization meeting of Directors and Incorporators of the said Corporation.

    Furthermore, we hereby agree that said meeting shall be held at   o'clock   .m. on

, 19 , at the following location:_____

_____.

    We do hereby affix our names to show our waiver of notice of said meeting.

Dated:

_____   _____

_____   _____

WARRANTY BILL OF SALE

BE IT KNOWN, that for good consideration, and in payment of the sum of $,
the receipt and sufficiency of which is acknowledged, the undersigned

of   (Seller) hereby sells and transfers to

                    of

(Buyer) and its successors and assigns forever, the following described chattels and personal
property.

      Seller warrants to Buyer it has good and marketable title to said property, full authority to
sell and transfer said property, and that said property is sold free of all liens, encumbrances,
liabilities and adverse claims of every nature and description whatsoever.

      Seller further warrants to Buyer that it will fully defend, protect, indemnify and hold
harmless the Buyer and its lawful successors and assigns from any adverse claim thereto.

      Said assets are otherwise sold in "as is" condition and where presently located.

      Signed this   day of   , 19   .

In the presence of:

_____   _____

Witness   Seller

                                                               _____

                                                               Address

                                                               _____

WARRANTY DEED

For good consideration, we
of   , County of   , State of
, hereby bargain, deed and convey to   of
, County of   , State of
, the following described land in   County, free and clear
with WARRANTY COVENANTS; to wit:

Grantor, for itself and its heirs, hereby covenants with Grantee, its heirs, and assigns, that Grantor is lawfully seized in fee simple of the above-described premises; that it has a good right to convey; that the premises are free from all encumbrances; that Grantor and its heirs, and all persons acquiring any interest in the property granted, through or for Grantor, will, on demand of Grantee, or its heirs or assigns, and at the expense of Grantee, its heirs or assigns, execute any instrument necessary for the further assurance of the title to the premises that may be reasonably required; and that Grantor and its heirs will forever warrant and defend all of the property so granted to Grantee, its heirs, and assigns, against every person lawfully claiming the same or any part thereof.

Being the same property conveyed to the Grantors by deed of   , dated
, 19   .

WITNESS the hands and seal of said Grantors this   day of   , 19   .

_____

Grantor

_____

Grantor

STATE OF   }
COUNTY OF
On   before me,   , personally appeared
, personally known to me (or proved to me on the basis of satisfactory evidence) to be the person(s) whose name(s) is/are subscribed to the within instrument and acknowledged to me that he/she/they executed the same in his/her/their authorized capacity(ies), and that by his/her/their signature(s) on the instrument the person(s), or the entity upon behalf of which the person(s) acted, executed the instrument.

WITNESS my hand and official seal.

Signature_____

Affiant _____Known _____Unknown
ID Produced_____

(Seal)

WITHHELD DELIVERY NOTICE

Date:

To:

Dear

Reference is made to your order for certain goods under date of   , 19   ,

as per your Purchase Order No.

We are withholding delivery for the reason(s) checked:

_____ Overdue balance of $_____must first be paid.

_____ Required payment of $_____has not been made.

_____ You previously withdrew your order.

_____ You failed to furnish required shipping instructions.

_____ Certain goods are back ordered and shipment will be made in single lot.

_____ Other

Please respond to this notice so we may fulfill your order without further delay or inconvenience.

Very truly,

_____

WRITTEN UNANIMOUS CONSENT IN LIEU OF A MEETING

The undersigned, being the holders of all of the outstanding shares of

Corporation entitled to vote at a meeting of shareholders, do hereby

consent to the following resolution adopted by the Board of Directors of

Corporation taken on _____ , 19 :

Dated:

Signed:_____

_____

_____

GLOSSARY

—A—

Acceptance of Claim—
Collection agency agreement.

Accident Claim Notice—
Notice to insurance agency of claim due to an accident.

Acknowledgement of Modified Terms—
Response to changes in a contract.

Addendum to Contract—
Adds or modifies terms to a contract.

Address Change Notice—
Notifies all parties of a change of address.

Affidavit—
A statement of fact.

Affidavit of Lost Stock Certificate—
A notarized statement attesting the loss of a stock certificate.

Affidavit of Mailing of Notice of Annual Meeting—
A notarized statement attesting mailing of notices.

Affidavit of Notice by Mail—
A notarized statement attesting to the receipt of notice.

Affidavit of Publication of Certificate– Fictitious or Assumed Name—
A notarized statement attesting publication of certificate in newspaper.

Agreement of Waiver of Right of Inheritance—
A beneficiary under a will gives up their right to inherit.

Agreement to Assume Obligation Secured by Mortgage—
Agreement to make payments for the mortgagor (borrower).

Agreement to Convert Separate Property into Community Property—
A marital agreement to combine the property of both spouses.

Agreement to Extend Performance Date—
Written notice to contractor extending time to complete project.

Agreement to Extend Period of Option—
Written notice to option holder extending time to exercise option.

Agreement to Lease—
Usually used for commercial property.

Agreement to Purchase Stock—
Written contract outlining terms of buying stock.

Agreement to Sell Personal Property—
Usually used for the sale of any kind of property other than real estate.

Amendment to Lease—
Written changes to lease terms.

Arbitration Agreement—
To settle a dispute using a unbiased third party.

Articles of Incorporation—
Sets up a corporation.

Assignment by Endorsing on Lease—
To sublease commercial property.

Assignment of Accounts Receivable with Non-Recourse—
Turns over uncollected income to a third party with no guarantee of payment.

Assignment of Accounts Receivable with Recourse—
Relinquishes uncollected income to a third party who guarantees payment.

Assignment of Assets—
Gives control of assets to a third party.

Assignment of Bank Account—
Gives the contents of a bank account to a third party.

Assignment of Contract—
Turns over contract obligation to a third party who must fulfill those obligations.

Assignment of Copyright—
Gives away the rights to a copyright to a third party.

Assignment of Damage Claim—
Gives right to claim damages to a third party.

Assignment of Insurance Policy—
Gives benefits of policy to third party.

Assignment of Lease—
Turns over lease to a third party.

Assignment of Money Due—
Gives a third party the right to collect money owed.

Assignment of Mortgage—
Transfers the right to collect mortgage owed to a third party.

Assignment of Option—
Transfers the right to exercise option to third party.

Assignment of Trademark—
Gives third party the right to use Trademark.

Authorization to Release Confidential Information—
Gives company or individual approval to issue confidential information.

Authorization to Release Credit Information—
Gives company approval to issue information about your credit to others.

Authorization to Release Employment Information—
Approves the release of job information.

Authorization to Release Information—
Gives general approval to release information.

Authorization to Release Medical Information—
Used to notify doctors, hospitals, insurance companies of approval to release medical information.

Authorization to Return Goods—
Seller approves return of goods shipped to buyer.

Bad Check Notice—
Company holding bad check notifies check writer to pay in cash.

Balloon Note—
Agreement to borrow money and repay in lump sum.

Bill of Sale—
Document showing all parties to a sale, the type of property sold, and the price.

Breach of Contract Notice—
Notice sent to party of contract specifying the terms violated.

Bulk Sales Affidavit—
A notarized statement attesting the sale of a business' entire inventory.

Bulk Sales Notice—
Sent to creditors to notify them of the sale of a business' entire inventory.

Cancellation of Home Solicitation Contract—
Notice by buyer to seller.

Cancellation of Stop-Payment Order—
Check writer sends to bank.

Certificate of Amendment—
A document that certifies a change in a corporation's Articles of Incorporation.

Certificate of Corporate Resolution—
Certifies the adoption of a resolution by the corporation's stockholders and directors.

Certificate of Limited Partnership—
Certifies the liability of the partners.

Certificate of Sale of Business Under an Assumed Name—Certifies the sale of a business.

Certificate of Termination of Business Under a Fictitious or Assumed Name—
Certifies that a business has ceased operations.

Certificate of Withdrawal of Partner from Business—
Certifies that a partner has ceased involvement with a business.

Change of Beneficiary—
Notifies insurance company of a new person to benefit from your policy.

Change of Beneficiary Notice—
Notifies the beneficiary that they will no longer benefit from insurance policy.

Change of Loss Payee Notice—
Changes beneficiary of a casualty insurance policy.

Change Work Order—
Written revisions to a contract to perform specific tasks, such as construction of a building.

Check Stop-Payment—
Request to bank to not honor a particular check.

Child Guardianship Consent Form—
Appoints a guardian and specifies their powers.

Claim of Lien—
Notifies third parties of a monetary interest in property where work was performed.

Codicil—
Adds or changes a paragraph in a will.

Cohabitation Agreement—
Outlines rights of two parties seeking to live together.

Commercial Lease—
Agreement to rent commercial property.

Conditional Sale Agreement—
Seller reserves title until buyer pays for goods.

Conduct of Business Under Fictitious or Assumed Name—
An application to do business in a particular state, usually filed with the Secretary of State.

Confidentiality Agreement—
Agreement between two or more parties to keep certain information secret.

Confirmation of Verbal Order—
Letter from buyer confirming placement of order with seller.

Consent for Drug/Alcohol Screen Testing—
Agreement by employee authorizing company to take tests.

Consent to Assignment—
Owner of property or contract agrees to transfer of rights to a third party.

Consent to Partial Assignment—
Owner of contract or property agrees to partial transfer of rights or obligations.

Consignment Agreement—
Agreement to buy goods and sell on consignment.

Consulting Services Agreement—
Defines tasks to be completed by consultant.

Consumer Loan Agreement—
Basic note to borrow money using collateral.

Contract—
Basic agreement between two or more parties.

Contractor Agreement—
Basic agreement to perform construction.

Corporate Acknowledgement—
A notarized statement attesting to action taken by corporation's board of directors.

Covenant Not to Sue—
Agreement not to take legal action.

Credit Information Request—
Company request for credit information from potential customer.

Credit Interchange—
Response to request for credit information from another company on a potential customer.

Creditor's Affidavit—
A notarized statement attesting to indebtedness.

Damaged Goods Acceptance—
Letter from buyer to seller accepting damaged goods.

Debt Acknowledgement—
Debtor's statement admitting indebtedness to creditor.

Debt Re-Affirmation—
Statement reassuring creditor that debtor intends to repay debt.

Declaration of Trust—
Trustee's promises to beneficiary regarding property held in trust.

Defective Goods Notice—
Notice to seller of buyer's decision to reject delivery of defective goods.

Demand for Contribution—
One party asks another party to contribute to a payment affected by a contract.

Demand for Delivery—
Buyer demands delivery from seller for goods ordered and paid for.

Demand for Inspection—
Stockholder's request for access to corporate books.

Demand for Payment—
Creditor's request for payment on past due account.

Demand for Rent—
Landlord's request for tenant to pay rent.

Demand Note—
Borrower's promise to repay loan upon demand.

Demand on Guarantor for Payment—
Creditor's demand for payment from guarantor when debtor defaults.

Demand Promissory Note—
Borrower promises to repay loan upon demand.

Demand to Acknowledge Shipping Date—
Buyer's request for seller to specify shipping date.

Demand to Endorser for Payment—
Check or note holder's demand to endorser to pay face amount.

Demand to Pay Promissory Note—
Creditor's demand to debtor to pay note.

Direct Deposit Authorization—
Employee's response to company's request for direct deposit payroll.

Discharge of Mortgage—
Mortgage holder's release of mortgagor.

Disciplinary Notice—
Company's warning to employee regarding behavior.

Dishonored Check Placed for Bank Collection—
Company's request to bank to place bad check for collection.

Disputed Account Settlement—
Debtor's agreement with creditor on disputed account.

Dissolution of Corporation Certificate—
Certifies a corporation is no longer in business.

Durable Power of Attorney—
Appoints another to act on behalf of grantor, person signing document.

Employee Agreement on Inventions and Patents—
Waiver of rights to any inventions.

Employee Covenant: Expense Recovery—
Agreement to repay any disallowed **expenses.**

Employee Non-Compete Agreement—
Contract to refrain from competing with employer.

Employee Non-Disclosure Agreement—
Contract to keep company information confidential.

Employee Warning—
Notice of unsatisfactory work performance.

Employment Agreement—
Terms under which employee agrees to work for company.

Escrow Agreement—
Establishes the disposition of funds set aside in a purchase and sales agreement.

Exceptions to Purchase Order—
Sets down exclusions to purchase order.

Exclusive Right to Sell—
Agreement giving broker the sole privilege to sell real property.

Exercise of Option—
Written notice of decision to accept option.

Extension of Agreement—
Contract that extends a previous agreement.

Extension of Lease—
Contract that extends a previous lease.

—F—

Fictitious or Assumed Name Certificate by a Corporation—
Certifies a corporation operating a business under a particular name.

Fictitious or Assumed Name Certificate by an Individual—
Certifies an individual operating a business under a particular name.

Fictitious or Assumed Name Certificate by Partners—
Certifies a partnership operating a business under a particular name.

Final Notice Before Legal Action—
Letter sent to individual or company with whom you have a dispute.

Final Warning Before Dismissal—
Letter sent to employee as warning prior to termination.

—G—

General Agreement—
Basic agreement between two or more parties.

General Assignment—
Basic document transferring right and title to a specific item or contract from one person to another.

General Power of Attorney—
Appoints another to act in your behalf.

General Release—
Discharges an entity from any claims arising from a specific act or transaction.

Gift in Advance of Testamentary Bequest—
Transfers assets from one party to another prior to the former's death.

Gift to Minor Under Uniform Gift to Minors Act—
Transfers property to a minor under a custodian's care until child reaches adulthood.

Grant of Right to Use Name—
Grants one party the right to use the name of another.

Guaranty—
Third party guarantees payment of another's debts to induce creditor to extend credit.

Guaranty of Rents—
Third party guarantee's payment of another's rent to induce landlord to lease.

—I—

Incumbency Certificate—
Certifies the officers of a corporation as of a specific date.

Indemnity Agreement—
Releases a party from any liability arising from a specific act or transaction.

Independent Contractor Agreement—
Sets down terms of independent contract.

Individual Acknowledgement—
A notarized statement attesting to an individual's identity.

Information Request on Disputed Charge—
Letter to seller from buyer requesting information on recent charges.

Insurance Claim Notice—
Letter to insurance company detailing claim.

Invitation to Quote Price of Goods—
Letter requesting price quote on goods.

Irrevocable Proxy—
A notarized document appointing another to vote and act on shareholder's behalf at shareholder's meeting.

—L—

Landlord's and Tenant's Mutual Release—
Document that releases both parties from any claims arising from tenancy.

Landlord's Notice to Terminate Tenancy—
Letter to tenant giving notice of landord's decision to end lease.

Landlord's Notice to Vacate—
Letter specifying date tenant is to vacate premises.

Last Will and Testament—
Sets down the distribution of property upon death.

Lease Termination Agreement—
Mutual agreement to cancel lease before original termination.

Letter Requesting Authorization to Release Credit Information—
Letter from company to potential customer seeking approval to obtain credit information.

Limited Guaranty—
Third party agrees to a maximum liability of debt for another.

Lost Credit Card Notice—
Letter to credit card company from cardholder requesting halt in credit.

—M—

Mailing List Name Removal Request—
Letter to company requesting removal of name from mailing list.

Minutes, First Meeting of Shareholders —
Records actions of shareholders at first meeting.

Minutes of Combined Meeting of Stockholders and Directors—
Records actions of stockholders and directors.

Minutes of Directors' Meeting—
Records actions of directors.

Minutes of Special Meeting of Stockholders—
Records actions of stockholders at special meeting.

Mortgage Bond—
A promise from borrower to repay lender a principal sum plus interest.

Mortgage Deed—
Borrower gives mortgage covenants to lender in consideration of loan.

Mutual Cancellation of Contract—
All parties agree to cancel specified contract.

Mutual Releases—
All parties discharge one another from any claim arising from specified contract.

—N—

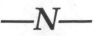

Non-Compete Agreement—
One party agrees not to compete with the business of another.

Nondisclosure Agreement—
Contract between consultant and client to keep proprietary information secret.

Notice of Assignment—
Letter notifying debtor or obligor that account or contract has been transferred to a third party.

Notice of Assignment to Obligor—
Letter notifying obligor of transfer of contract.

Notice of Change in Rent—
Letter from landlord advising tenant of a change in rent.

Notice of C.O.D. Terms—
Letter from seller notifying buyer of C.O.D. Terms.

Notice of Debt Assignment—
Letter to debtor advising of transfer of obligation.

Notice of Default by Assignee to Obligor—
Notice by assignee to debtor of default.

Notice of Default in Payment—
Letter to debtor advising payment is past due.

Notice of Default on Promissory Note—
Letter to debtor demanding payment and warning of collection.

Notice of Dismissal—
Letter advising employee of company's decision to terminate position.

Notice of Disputed Account—
Letter from customer disputing charges.

Notice of Election to Cancel—
Letter informing party of specified contract of other party's decision to cancel.

Notice of Forfeiture—
Letter informing party of specified contract of other party's decision to forfeit contract.

Notice of Intent to Repossess Due to Default—
Lender's notice to borrower advising of intent to repossess property affected by default of specified contract.

Notice of Lease—
Provides public notice of an impending lease agreement.

Notice of Organization Meeting of Incorporators and Directors—
Advises incorporators and directors of meeting.

Notice of Private Sale of Collateral—
Advises debtor of private sale of property pursuant to Uniform Commercial Code.

Notice of Public Sale of Collateral—
Advises debtor of public sale of property pursuant to Uniform Commercial Code.

Notice of Purchase Money Security Interest—
Letter sent to lienholder advising of priority claim to property.

Notice of Rent Arrears—
Letter advising tenant of past due rent.

Notice of Rescission—
Letter advising party of undoing of a contract, more than a termination.

Notice of Results of Public Sale—
Letter to debtor stating the outcome of the sale.

Notice of Termination Due to Work Rules Violation—
Letter advising employee of discharge.

Notice of Unpaid Invoice—
Letter to customer detailing payments.

Notice of Wrongful Refusal to Accept Delivery—
Letter from seller advising buyer of breach of purchase contract.

Notice to Cancel Back-Ordered Goods—
Letter from buyer advising seller of decision to cancel order for back-ordered goods.

Notice to Cancel Delayed Good—
Letter from buyer advising seller of decision to cancel order because of delay.

Notice to Correct Credit Report—
Letter to credit reporting agency detailing inaccurate information.

Notice to Directors of Special Meeting—
Letter advising directors of special meeting.

Notice to Exercise Lease Option—
Letter from tenant advising landlord of decision to exercise option.

Notice to Landlord to Make Repairs—
Letter advising landlord to repair premises.

Notice to Pay Rent or Quit—
Letter advising tenant to pay past due rent or vacate premises.

Notice to Purchaser of Breach of Option—
Letter from seller advising buyer of violating option terms.

Notice to Reclaim Goods—
Letter from seller advising buyer to return delivered goods.

Notice to Redirect Payments—
Letter advising debtor to pay a third party.

Notice to Remedy Default by Tenant—
Letter from landlord advising tenant to comply with lease terms.

Notice to Shareholders of Annual Meeting—
Letter advising shareholders of annual meeting.

Notice to Stop Credit Charge—
Letter from credit cardholder instructing company to withhold payment of specified charge.

Notice to Stop Goods in Transit—
Letter advising shipping company to return goods to seller.

Notice to Tenant to Make Repairs—
Letter from landlord advising tenant to repair premises under terms of lease.

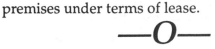

Offer to Purchase Real Estate—
Agreement presented to owner suggesting price buyer is willing to pay.

Open Listing Realty Agreement—
Contract between owner and broker to pay commission if broker finds buyer.

Option to Purchase—
Contract between owner and buyer specifying time period in which to exercise option.

Option to Purchase Stock—
Agreement specifying time period in which to exercise option.

Organ Donation of—
A document that specifies the wishes of an organ donor.

Partial Release of Lien—
Agreement by person or company that performed work or furnished materials to release property owner from a portion of the amount due.

Partial Shipment Request—
Letter advising buyer of seller's intent to ship a partial order.

Partnership Acknowledgement—
A notarized statement admitting to the act or actions of a partnership.

Partnership Agreement—
Contract between two parties to form a business.

Past Due Reminder—
Letter reminding debtor of overdue payment.

Payment Inquiry—
Letter that asks debtor to explain reasons for non-payment.

Payment on Specific Accounts—
Letter specifying to creditor what items shall be paid with enclosed check.

Payment on Written Instrument—
Receipt for payment on account for note.

Payroll Deduction Authorization—
Form authorizing company to make specific deductions from an employee's paycheck.

Permission to Use Copyrighted Material—
Agreement by copyright holder to allow someone to use the copyright.

Permission to Use Quote or Personal Statement—
Agreement granting the use of spoken or written words.

Personal Property Rental Agreement—
Agreement between owner and renter for the use of personal property, for example, a boat.

Pledge of Personal Property—
Agreement to deliver specific property to creditor to secure payment of a debt.

Pledge of Shares of Stock—
Agreement to deliver shares of stock to creditor to secure payment of a debt.

Polygraph Consent—
Agreement by employee to submit to a polygraph examination.

Postnuptial Property Agreement—
Agreement between spouses following marriage defining their rights to the separate, joint and community property of the parties.

Power of Attorney Delegating Parental Authority—
Appoints a custodian for minor child and specifies custodian's powers.

Power of Attorney Revocation—
Revokes the appointment of another to act on behalf of your interests.

Premarital Agreement—
Specifies each party's rights to property held before marriage and its disposition in the event of separation or divorce.

Presentment by Mail—
Demand of payment by mail by the holder of a note.

Privacy Release—
Grants permission to use name, picture, portrait or photograph in all forms of media without prior inspection.

Product Defect Claim—
Letter from wholesaler or retailer advising manufacturer of defect claim.

Product Defect Notice—
Letter from customer advising manufacturer, distributor or seller of a defective product.

Product Warranty Claim—
Letter requesting repair or replacement of defective product under warranty.

Promissory Note—
A promise to pay a principal sum plus interest.

Proposal to Buy a Business—
Letter advising owner of interest in buying business.

Proxy to Vote Corporate Shares—
Appoints another to vote your shares on behalf of you.

Purchase Requirement Agreement—
Contract to purchase a specified quantity of goods during a specific period.

Purchaser's Assignment of Option—
Transfers option rights to a third party.

—Q—

Quitclaim Bill of Sale—
Sale agreement that gives up any claims to property by seller without warranties.

Quitclaim Deed—
A deed that gives up all right, title, interest and claim in a specific property without warranties.

—R—

Receipt—
Basic receipt for payment that can be used for full or partial payment.

Receipt for Balance of Account—
Used when balance of account is paid.

Receipt in Full—All Demands—
Used when amount owed is paid in full.

Receipt in Full By an Agent—
Used when a third party makes full payment for a debtor.

Receipt in Full by an Agent to an Agent —
Use when a third party representing the creditor accepts full payment from a third party representing the debtor.

Receipt of Note for Collection—
Agent agrees to collect payment on note and retain a percentage for effort.

Receipt on Account for Goods to be Delivered—
Receipt for payment in advance of delivery.

Receipt on Account for Partial Payment —
Receipt for partial payment on account balance.

Referral of Claim for Collection —
Letter to Collection Agency turning over account for collection.

Refused Credit Information Request—
Letter asking company to explain reasons for denying credit.

Rejected Goods Notice—
Letter from buyer advising seller of reasons for rejection.

Release and Waiver of Option Rights—
Releases option holder of all claim, right and interest in the option.

Release of Breach of Lease by Tenant—
Releases tenant of any liability due to breach of lease.

Release of Mechanic's Liens—
Releases property owner of any and all liens to date.

Release of Mortgage—
Releases mortgagor from mortgage, either because debt has been fully paid or discharged.

Release of Mortgage by a Corporation—
Corporation releases mortgagor from mortgage.

Release—Individual—
Releases all claims, judgments, demands, actions from one party against another.

Renewal of Fictitious or Assumed Name Certificate—
Certifies the renewal of a certificate to do business.

Renewal of Notice of Assignment of Accounts—
Notifies interested parties of renewal of transfer of accounts to third party.

Request for Bank Credit Reference—
Letter to bank requesting reference.

Request for Credit Interchange—
Inquiry to another company for credit information on a potential customer.

Request for Credit Report—
Letter to reporting agency for full and complete disclosure of credit file.

Request for Reference—
Letter to potential employee's previous employer requesting reference.

Request Under Freedom of Information Act—
Letter to any government agency that may keep files on individuals.

Reservation of Corporate Name—
Request to reserve corporate name prior to incorporating.

Reservation of Multiple Corporate Names—
Request to reserve corporate names prior to incorporating.

Residential Lease—
Agreement to rent residential property.

Residential Rental Application— Application for rental of residential property.

Resignation—
Standard resignation letter used to resign from a corporate or company position.

Resignation of Trustee—
Standard resignation letter used to resign as trustee of a trust.

Return of Claim as Noncollectible—
Letter from collection agency advising client of noncollectible claim.

Revocable Living Trust—
Establishes a trust to hold, manage and invest property for the benefit of the settlor.

Revocable Proxy—
Appoints a proxy to vote on behalf of a shareholder, who retains the right to revoke said appointment.

Revocation of Guaranty—
Letter notifying creditor of guarantor's decision to revoke guarantee.

Revocation of Power of Attorney—
A notarized statement by principal rescinding appointment of power of attorney.

Revocation of Proxy—
A notarized statement by shareholder revoking appointment of proxy.

Sale on Approval Acknowledgement —
Letter from seller to buyer admitting goods were shipped for sale on approval.

Sales Representative Agreement—
Contract between company and sales representative to sell company's products or services.

Second Notice of Overdue Account—
Letter to debtor requesting payment of past due account.

Security Agreement—
Agreement between debtor and secured party putting up property to secure payment of specific obligations.

Sight Draft—
An instrument payable upon presentment.

Specific Guaranty—
Agreement by a third party to guarantee the payment of a specific obligation.

Specific Power of Attorney—
Appoints an attorney-in-fact to perform a specific act on behalf of the grantor.

Specific Release—
Release from any and all claims, contracts, suits, actions or liabilities specifically arising from a defined act or transaction.

Statement of Wishes—
Document that outlines actions to be taken after a person dies.

Stock Subscription—
Request to purchase shares of a corporation at a given price.

Stock Transfer—
Sale agreement of stock in a corporation.

Stockholders Redemption Agreement—
Contract between stockholder and corporation detailing stock redemption procedures.

Sublease—
Agreement between tenant, landlord and subtenant to sublet premises currently under lease to tenant that retains tenant's liability.

Surety Bond—
An agreement that for a specified sum assures the completion of a contract.

Tenant's Notice to Exercise Purchase Option—
Letter to landlord accepting option to purchase.

Tenant's Notice to Terminate Tenancy—
Letter advising landlord of decision to cancel lease.

Three Day Notice to Vacate for Non-Payment of Rent—
Letter giving tenant three days to move out or face eviction.

Time Note—
A promise to pay principal and interest by a specific date.

Trip Permission—
Authorizes minor to take a trip and appoints an adult to render medical care if necessary.

—U—

Unsolicited Idea Acknowledgement—
Company's reply to receiving idea.

—V—

Verification of Education—
Employer's request to verify education of potential employee.

Verification of Licensure—
License holder's request for verification of registration.

Waiver and Assumption of Risk—
Customer's agreement to hold seller harmless from any liability or risk in using product or service.

Waiver of Lien—
Lienholder releases all right to claim any liens for work done or material furnished.

Waiver of Notice Combined Meeting—
Stockholder release of corporation from required meeting notice.

Waiver of Notice of Annual Meeting by Individual Shareholder—
Stockholder release of corporation from required meeting notice.

Waiver of Notice of Director's Meeting—
Director release of corporation from required meeting notice.

Waiver of Notice of Organization Meeting of Incorporators and Directors—
Incorporators and directors release of corporation from required meeting notice.

Warranty Bill of Sale—
Sale of property warranted with good and marketable title.

Warranty Deed—
Land conveyed with warranty covenants providing assurance of title.

Withheld Delivery Notice—
Letter advising buyer of reasons seller has not delivered goods.

Written Unanimous Consent in Lieu of a Meeting—
Corporate document that provides stockholder approval of action without meeting.

Stock No.: LA101
$24.95 8.5" x 11"
500 pages Soft cover
ISBN 1-56382-101-X

The E•Z Legal Advisor

The book that saves legal fees every time it's opened.

Here, in *The E•Z Legal Advisor*, are fast answers to 90% of the legal questions anyone is ever likely to ask, such as:

- How can I control my neighbor's pet?
- Can I change my name?
- When is a marriage common law?
- When should I incorporate my business?
- Is a child responsible for his bills?
- Who owns a husband's gifts to his wife?
- How do I become a naturalized citizen?
- Should I get my divorce in Nevada?
- Can I write my own will?
- Who is responsible when my son drives my car?
- How does my uncle get a Green Card?
- What are the rights of a non-smoker?
- Do I have to let the police search my car?
- What is sexual harassment?
- When is euthanasia legal?
- What repairs must my landlord make?
- What's the difference between fair criticism and slander?
- When can I get my deposit back?
- Can I sue the federal government?
- Am I responsible for a drunk guest's auto accident?
- Is a hotel liable if it does not honor a reservation?
- Does my car fit the lemon law?

Whether for personal or business use, this 500-page information-packed book helps the layman safeguard his property, avoid disputes, comply with legal obligations, and enforce his rights. Hundreds of cases illustrate thousands of points of law, each clearly and completely explained.

E•Z LEGAL BOOKS®

E•Z Legal Guides...

**A complete "do-it-yourself" law library!
Available at your nearest bookstore,
or call 1-800-822-4566**

A collection of 12 user-friendly guides that take the consumer through routine legal procedures without a lawyer. Each guide is educational, easy to read and clear on when not to do it yourself. State-by-state laws and ready-to-complete forms are included where appropriate, and every guide contains the 10-page supplement "How To Save on Attorney Fees."

Last Will & Testament

Writing a will can be a simple matter. With the help of this book, the reader learns the process, follows the step-by-step directions, and fills out the forms provided. Contains a sample last will & testament as a guide, and supplementary forms to state last wishes, list personal information, and make final arrangements.

Stock No.: G107
$14.95 8.5" x 11"
96 pages Soft cover
ISBN 1-56382-407-8

Living Trust

For the informed consumer who wants to provide for loved ones, retain control of assets, avoid probate, and leave a lifetime of savings to heirs of his or her choosing. A living trust is a remarkable tool that does just that. This clear, step-by-step guide includes all the forms necessary to set up a living trust.

Stock No.: G105
$14.95 8.5" x 11"
110 pages Soft cover
ISBN 1-56382-405-1

Incorporation

This guide explains in laymen's terms how to incorporate without a lawyer. Includes the forms necessary and instructions for obtaining a state-specific "Certificate (or Articles) of Incorporation." Helps the sole proprietor or partnership to become a corporation, or the new business deciding where to incorporate.

Stock No.: G101
$14.95 8.5" x 11"
176 pages Soft cover
ISBN 1-56382-401-9

E·Z Legal Guides

- *Complete information*
- *Full instructions*
- *Do-it-yourself forms*
- *Only $14.95 each*

Living Will & Powers of Attorney

Dying with dignity is on the minds of every baby boomer and every boomer's parents. They are looking for information, for answers, for the forms they need to fill out now, while they are healthy. They'll find it all in one simple book, the *Guide to Living Will & Powers of Attorney*.

Stock No.: G106
$14.95 8.5" x 11"
128 pages Soft cover
ISBN 1-56382-406-X

Immigration

This simple guide explains the various ways America allows aliens to qualify for "green cards," offers step-by-step directions in the petition and application processes, and prepares immigrants to become naturalized citizens. An excellent reference book complete with federally required forms.

Stock No.: G113
$14.95 8.5" x 11"
176 pages Soft cover
ISBN 1-56382-413-2

Divorce

Spouses facing an amicable divorce shouldn't have to face off with contentious lawyers. This guide explains when a do-it-yourself divorce is appropriate, provides the forms necessary, takes the reader through the legal steps, and provides state-by-state information for filing for divorce.

Stock No.: G102
$14.95 8.5" x 11"
160 pages Soft cover
ISBN 1-56382-402-7

Credit Repair

Anyone can improve bad credit with the help of this guide. From discovering exactly what a credit report contains to challenging false information and turning unfavorable reports into glowing reports, it's all in this guide. Sample letters help the reader contact the right authorities and assert his or her consumer rights.

Stock No.: G103
$14.95 8.5" x 11"
176 pages Soft cover
ISBN 1-56382-403-5

Bankruptcy

How does someone file bankruptcy without adding to their debts? With the *E-Z Legal Guide to Bankruptcy*. Takes the confusion out of bankruptcy by taking the reader through the forms, the law, even the state and federal exemptions.

Stock No.: G100
$14.95 8.5" x 11"
128 pages Soft cover
ISBN 1-56382-400-0

Small Claims Court

The reader prepares for his day in court with this guide, which explains the process for the plaintiff and the defendant, offers options to an actual court case, and more. For anyone who has ever thought about taking someone to court.

Stock No.: G109
$14.95 8.5" x 11"
128 pages Soft cover
ISBN 1-56382-409-4

Employment Law

This is a handy reference for anyone with questions about hiring, wages and benefits, privacy, discrimination, injuries, sexual harassment, unions, and unemployment. Written in simple language from the perspectives of both the employer and the employee.

Stock No.: G112
$14.95 8.5",x 11"
112 pages Soft cover
ISBN 1-56382-412-4

Traffic Court

For most American drivers, traffic tickets are an annoying fact of life. But sometimes the motorist doesn't deserve the ticket. This guide tells how and why to fight a ticket, and how to handle a police stop, read a traffic ticket, and take it to court and win.

Stock No.: G110
$14.95 8.5" x 11"
112 pages Soft cover
ISBN 1-56382-410-8

Trademarks and Copyrights

When someone has a great idea and wants to protect it, this book provides the basics of copyright and trademark law: when to get a lawyer, when simply to fill out the right paperwork. Cuts through the volumes of technical information found elsewhere to provide what the layman must know.

Stock No.: G114
$14.95 8.5" x 11"
192 pages Soft cover
ISBN 1-56382-404-3

E•Z Legal® Software introduces Choice...

With five new E•Z Legal® Windows® programs that include both 3.5" Disks and state-of-the-art CD... so it's E•Z to install using either media.

User friendly package makes customers' buying decision E•Z. Written by attorneys, the forms are valid in all 50 states. Access specific information through convenient Help Files, then customize and print the forms you need, all right from your personal computer.

Divorce - Fact: Over half of today's marriages end in divorce. Get the facts about how to deal with the legalities on your own. Contains over 200 state-specific forms.
(UPC 053926441020 • ISBN 1-56382-013-7 • SW1102)

Credit Repair - If you think your credit is ruined forever, think again. Plug in our software, diagnose the problem, and you'll be in the black again in no time!
(UPC 053926441037 • ISBN 1-56382-012-9 • SW1103)

Incorporation - Should your business incorporate? We'll help answer this question, and if it's "yes," we'll provide all the information on how to protect your personal assets from business creditors.
(UPC 053926441013 • ISBN 1-56382-014-5 • SW1101)

Living Trust - Take steps now to avoid costly probate and eliminate one more worry for your family.
(UPC 053926441051 • ISBN 1-56382-016-1 • SW1105)

Last Will & Testament - Ensure your property goes to the heirs you choose. Includes state-specific Living Will and Power of Attorney for Healthcare forms!
(UPC 053926441075 • ISBN 1-56382-015-3 • SW1107)

For: WINDOWS 3.1 • WINDOWS 95 • WINDOWS NT WINDOWS FOR WORKGROUPS

System requirements:
386 or better, 3.5 disk drive or CD Drive, VGA card.
For Windows 3.1 and Windows for Workgroups:
4MB RAM (8 MB recommended);
7.5 MB free disk space
For Windows NT & Windows 95:
8MB RAM; 3.25MB free disk space

Designed for Microsoft Windows 95

E•Z LEGAL® SOFTWARE
...when you need it in writing!®

384 S. Military Trail
Deerfield Beach, FL 33442
1-800-822-4566

• Master carton: 10 • Weight per each: 1 lb. • Shipping Summer 1996 •

Microsoft, Windows, and the Windows logo are registered trademarks of Microsoft Corporation. Windows NT is a trademark of Microsoft Corporation

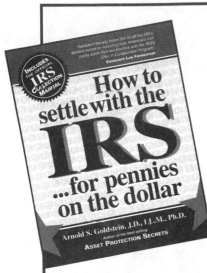

Asset Protection Secrets

This best seller has been featured on over 250 radio and TV shows!

Arnold S. Goldstein, Ph.D.

Asset Protection Secrets reveals all the little-known secrets and perfected strategies guaranteed to protect personal and business assets from financial disaster. This is a full resource guide packed solid with over 230 perfectly legal ways to:

- Become judgment proof.
- Go bankrupt and keep everything!
- Protect assets from IRS seizure.
- Avoid a lawsuit in today's lawsuit-crazy society.
- Leave assets to children so they're fully protected from creditors.
- Shelter property from the IRS, divorce, probate, and creditors.
- Safeguard a business from creditors.
- Shelter wages from attachment.
- Use offshore havens for ironclad financial secrecy and protection.

*D*r. *Arnold S. Goldstein is among a select group of distinguished experts recognized for his knowledge of tax and financial protection strategies. Featured on over 400 radio and television shows nationwide, he has authored more than 72 books on law, business and finance.*

Founder and President of Wealth$avers, an international financial planning and asset protection organization, Dr. Goldstein also conducts Asset Protection Secrets Seminars nationwide. He is Professor Emeritus at Northeastern University, and teaches asset protection strategies at several colleges and universities. He holds the degrees of Bachelor of Science, Master of Business Administration, Doctor of Jurisprudence, Master of Laws and Ph.D. in law and public policy. He is a member of the Massachusetts and federal bars as well as many professional, academic and civic organizations.

"Asset Protection Secrets is a complete encyclopedia of techniques and tactics to safeguard your assets under all circumstances."
Consumer Law Foundation

"The most important personal finance book this century."
Delray Press

"Asset Protection Secrets is awesome. It really shows people how to build a financial fortress around their wealth."
Robert Itzkow
Taxpayer's Assistance Corp.

**Newly revised edition...
Updated tax laws and more.**

OVER 80,000 COPIES IN PRINT

Stock No.: GAPS 100
$29.95 8.5" x 11"
360 pages Soft cover
ISBN 1-880539-004

 GARRETT PUBLISHING, INC.

The Business Doctor

Stock No.: TBD 300
$19.95 6" x 9"
326 pages Soft cover
ISBN 1-880539-25-X

The perfect prescription for the ailing business!

Arnold S. Goldstein, Ph.D.

The Business Doctor, loaded with fascinating examples of turnaround successes, is essential for every business owner. From a synopsis of why good companies fail through the step-by-step guide to resolving creditor problems, readers will benefit from its 19 chapters of indispensable, professional advice for owners or managers of financially troubled businesses. Chapters detail how to:

• Sidestep the 10 deadly business killers.
• Turn a business into a creditor-proof fortress.
• Find fast cash for a cash-starved business.
• Avoid Chapter 11.
• Transform losses into huge profits.
• Cash in by selling a troubled business.
...and more!

"Practical advice for those with failing or muddling businesses. This book teaches street fighting skills—your only hope."
Soundview Executive Book Summaries

"Dr. Arnold S. Goldstein has a brilliant reputation in the turnaround field. His strategies should be read by everyone with a faltering business."
Scott Dantuma, President Corporate Financial Recovery, Inc.

Buying and Selling a Business

Mark T. Lauer

Clearly written, precisely detailed, with simple guidelines, this book is for anyone considering buying or selling a business. It addresses critical questions such as: "Am I getting the best possible deal?" and "How much will I pay, and when?" The book covers these topics and more as it shows buyers and sellers how to:

• Evaluate and choose the right business.
• Effectively negotiate price and terms.
• Buy a franchised business...intelligently.
• Structure the deal for optimum tax, financial, and legal benefits.
• Find the best financing.
• Avoid the five major pitfalls for business buyers...and the six even bigger pitfalls for sellers.
...and more!

"This book is essential for anyone even thinking about buying or selling a business. It is jam-packed with solid information."
Ken MacKenzie Institute for Business Appraisal

THE BUSINESS BUYER'S/SELLER'S BIBLE

Stock No.: BSB 900
$24.95 8.5" x 11"
256 pages Soft cover
ISBN 1-880539-33-0

 GARRETT PUBLISHING, INC.

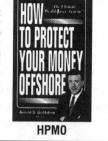

Debt Buster

Stock No.: DBT 600
$24.95   8.5" x 11"
256 pages Soft cover
ISBN 1-880539-26-8

Arnold S. Goldstein, Ph.D.

Debt Buster is a step-by-step guide to getting out of debt without bankruptcy, and managing personal finances efficiently. Here are the solutions for people coping with the daily stress of living from paycheck to paycheck and just making ends meet.

Featured on national television, the Debt Buster program has shown millions of Americans how to:

- Recognize the warning signals of problem debting.
- Protect themselves from bill collectors and negotiate with creditors.
- Use little-known laws to reduce debts.
- Eliminate debt without going broke.
- Avoid bankruptcy, foreclosures, and repossessions.
- Turn credit around, and obtain new credit.
- Protect assets from creditors
                     ...and much more!

Guaranteed Credit

Arnold S. Goldstein, Ph.D.

The perfect book for anyone with less-than-perfect credit. In fact, it's for anyone with no credit history, with any type of credit problem, rejected for credit or charge cards, starting over after bankruptcy, who wants to buy a house or car or apply for a bank loan, whose credit is overextended, or who wants more credit for his or her business!

Guaranteed Credit is a practical step-by-step system to establish, repair, or build credit from America's #1 "money doctor" and the man millions of Americans listen to for financial advice. More than a book on improving credit, *Guaranteed Credit* also explains how to get the best deal when you shop for credit. Finally, the author explains how not to abuse..and lose credit.

Features a publisher's **money-back guarantee** *if credit not improved after 90 days.*

Stock No.: GC 103
$24.95 8.5" x 11"
256 pages Soft cover
ISBN 1-880539-40-3

 GARRETT PUBLISHING, INC.